SAMURAI JACK

LOST WORLDS

IDW

[adult swim]
TM & © 2019 Cartoon Network

Facebook: **facebook.com/idwpublishing**
Twitter: **@idwpublishing**
YouTube: **youtube.com/idwpublishing**
Tumblr: **tumblr.idwpublishing.com**
Instagram: **instagram.com/idwpublishing**

ISBN: 978-1-68405-552-4   22 21 20 19   1 2 3 4

Cover Artist
Adam Bryce Thomas

Collection Edits by
Justin Eisinger
and **Alonzo Simon**

Collection Design by
Ron Estevez

Originally published as SAMURAI JACK: LOST WORLDS issues #1–4.

Chris Ryall, President, Publisher, & CCO
John Barber, Editor-In-Chief
Cara Morrison, Chief Financial Officer
Matt Ruzicka, Chief Accounting Officer
David Hedgecock, Associate Publisher
Jerry Bennington, VP of New Product Development
Lorelei Bunjes, VP of Digital Services
Justin Eisinger, Editorial Director, Graphic Novels & Collections
Eric Moss, Senior Director, Licensing and Business Development

Ted Adams and Robbie Robbins, IDW Founders

Special thanks to Marisa Marionakis, Brandon Lively, Elyse Salazar,
Janet No, Meagan Birney, and to Adult Swim.

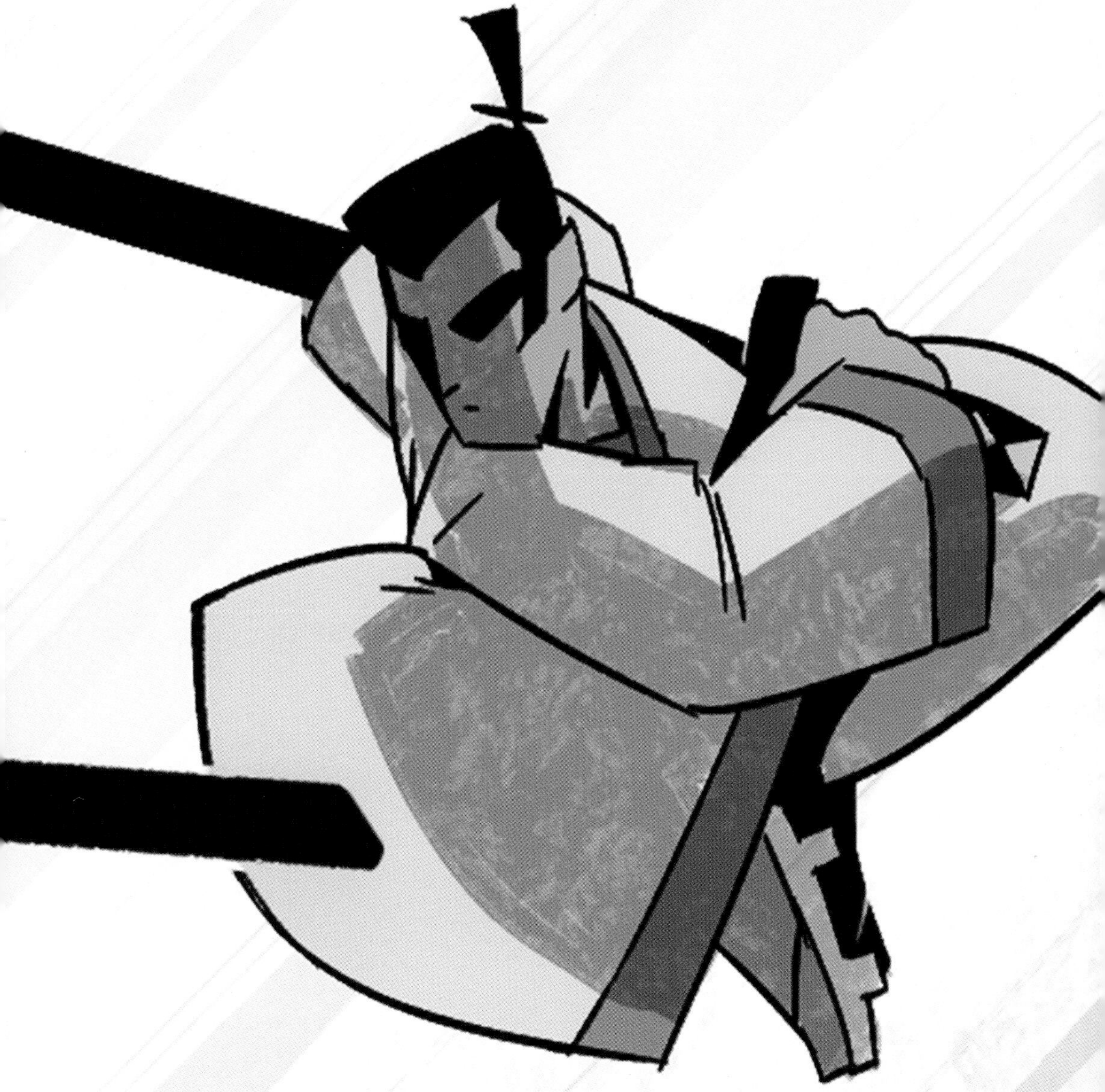

Written by **Paul Allor**

Art by **Adam Bryce Thomas**

Letters by **Christa Miesner**

Additional Letters by **Robbie Robbins**

Series Edits by **David Mariotte**

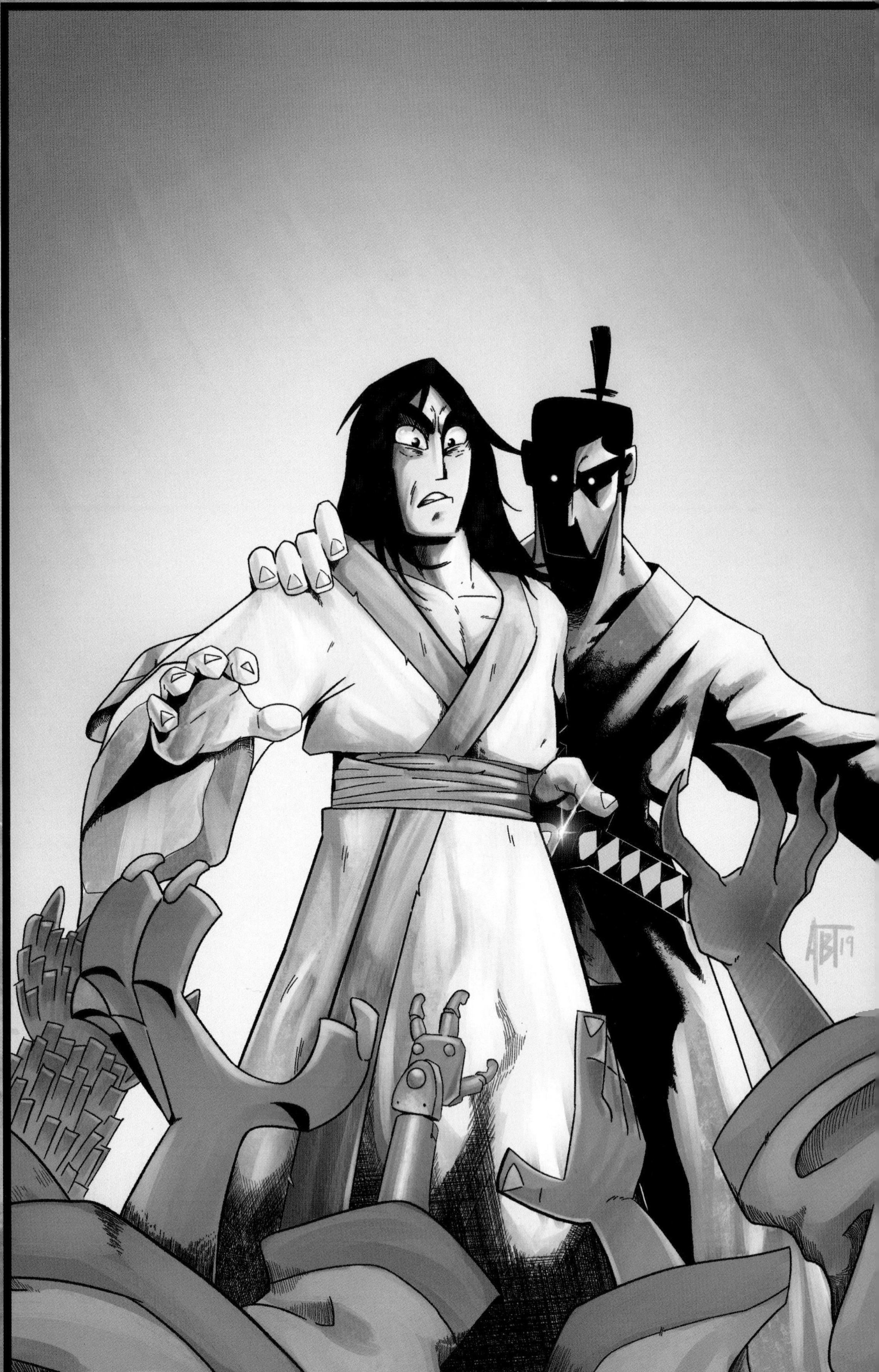
ABT '19
Art by Adam Bryce Thomas

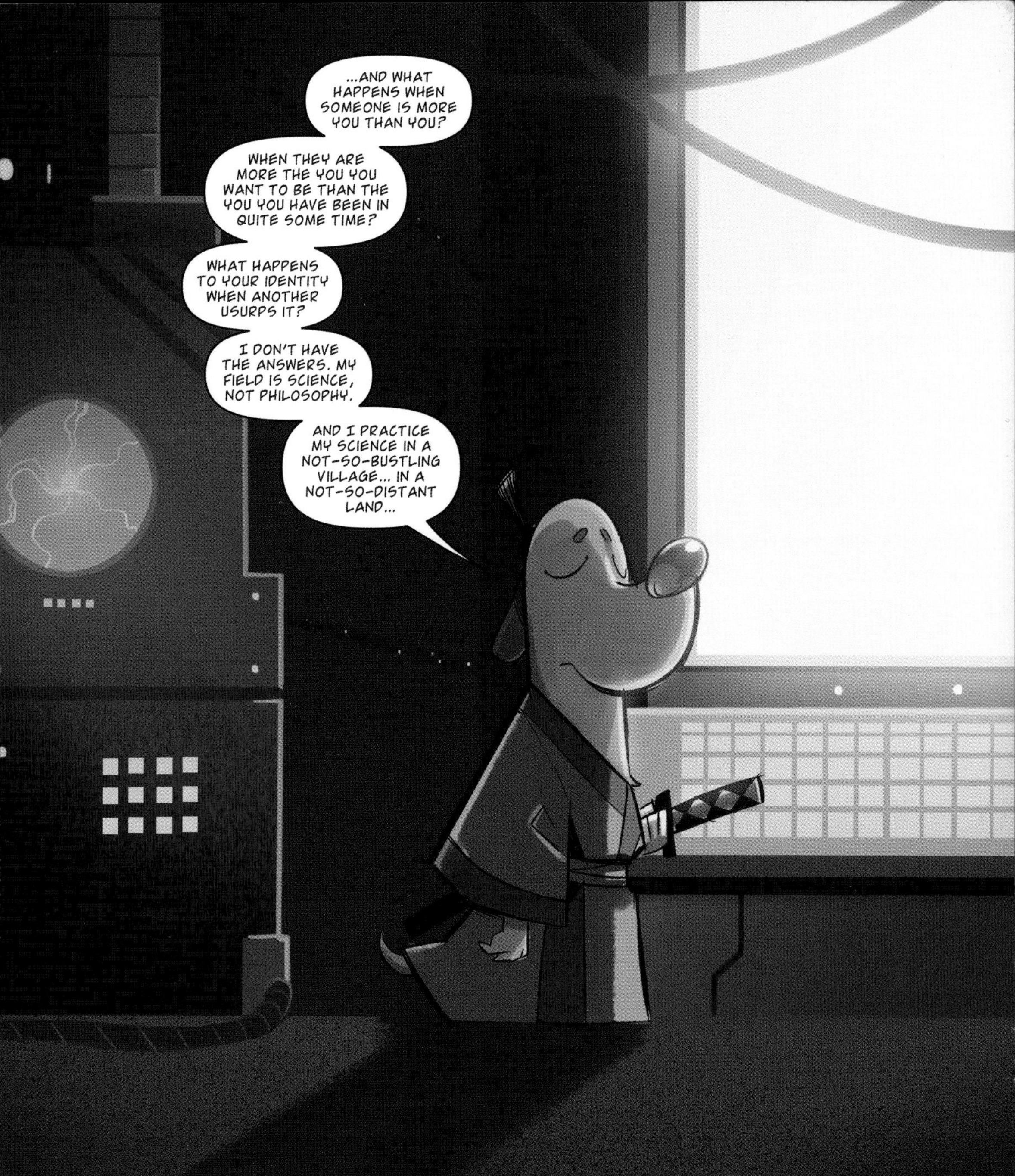
...AND WHAT HAPPENS WHEN SOMEONE IS MORE YOU THAN YOU?
WHEN THEY ARE MORE THE YOU YOU WANT TO BE THAN THE YOU YOU HAVE BEEN IN QUITE SOME TIME?
WHAT HAPPENS TO YOUR IDENTITY WHEN ANOTHER USURPS IT?
I DON'T HAVE THE ANSWERS. MY FIELD IS SCIENCE, NOT PHILOSOPHY.
AND I PRACTICE MY SCIENCE IN A NOT-SO-BUSTLING VILLAGE... IN A NOT-SO-DISTANT LAND...

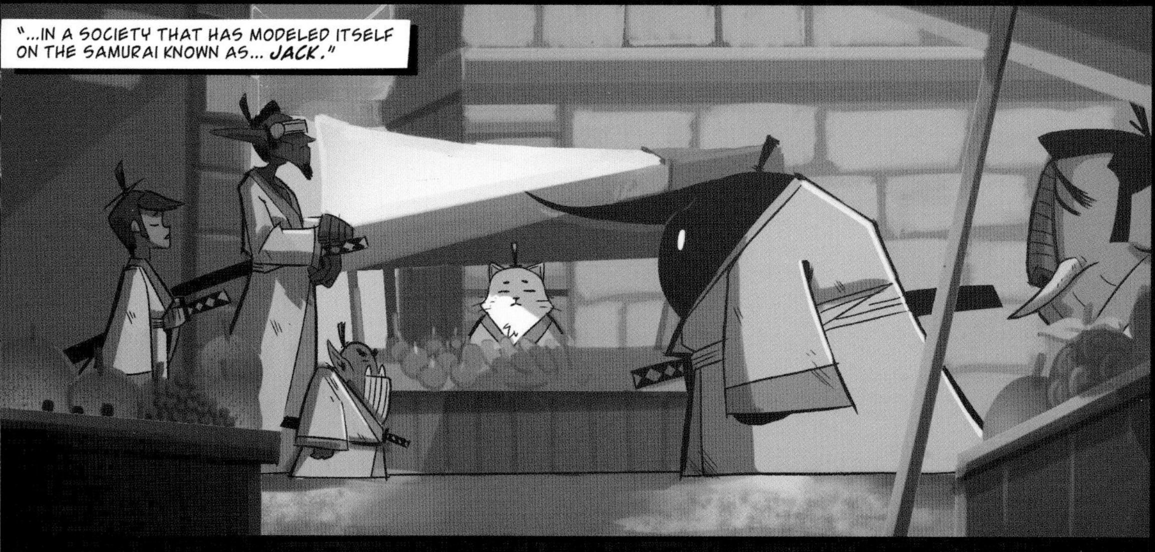
"...IN A SOCIETY THAT HAS MODELED ITSELF ON THE SAMURAI KNOWN AS... *JACK*."

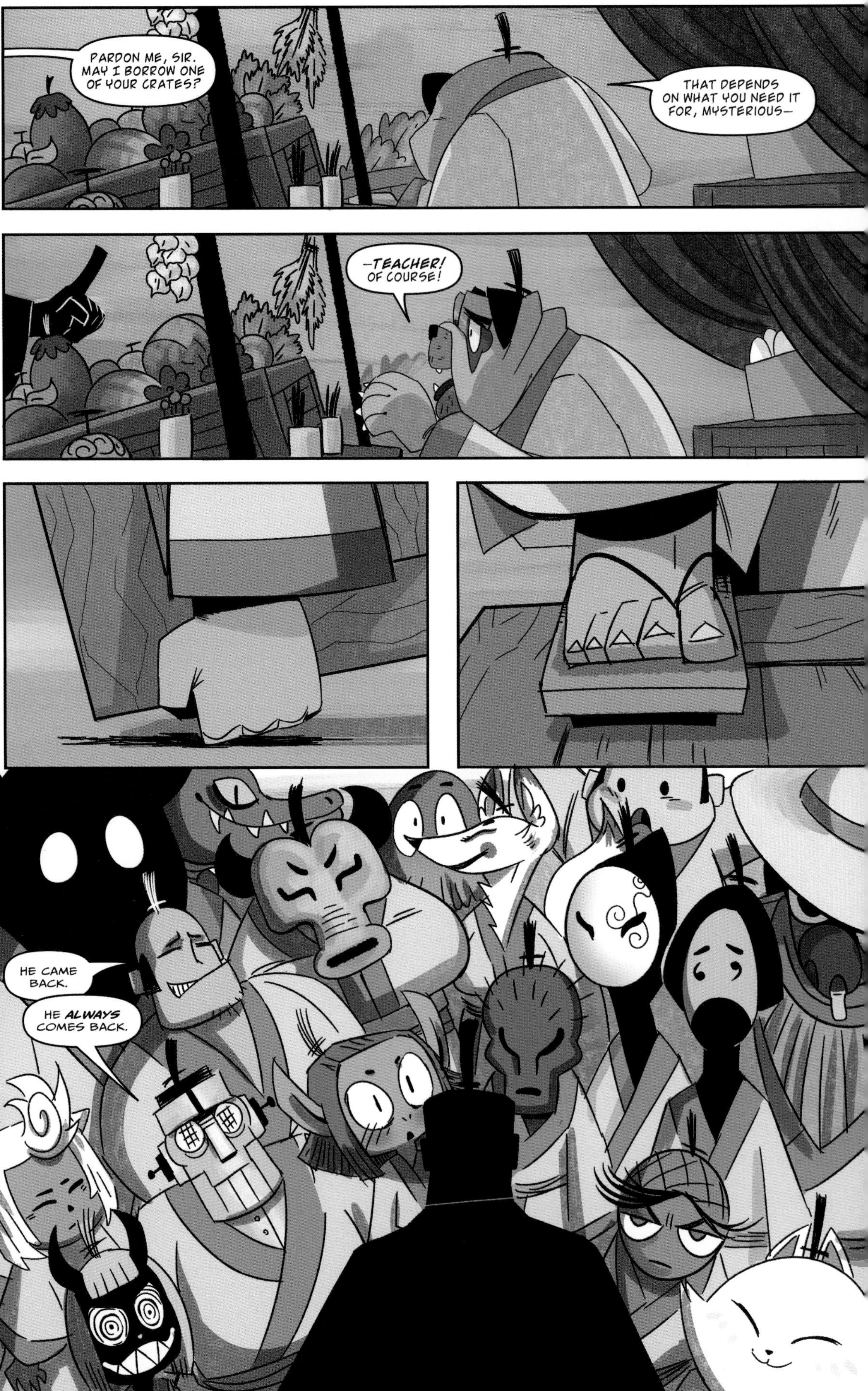
PARDON ME, SIR. MAY I BORROW ONE OF YOUR CRATES?
THAT DEPENDS ON WHAT YOU NEED IT FOR, MYSTERIOUS—
—TEACHER! OF COURSE!
HE CAME BACK.
HE ALWAYS COMES BACK.

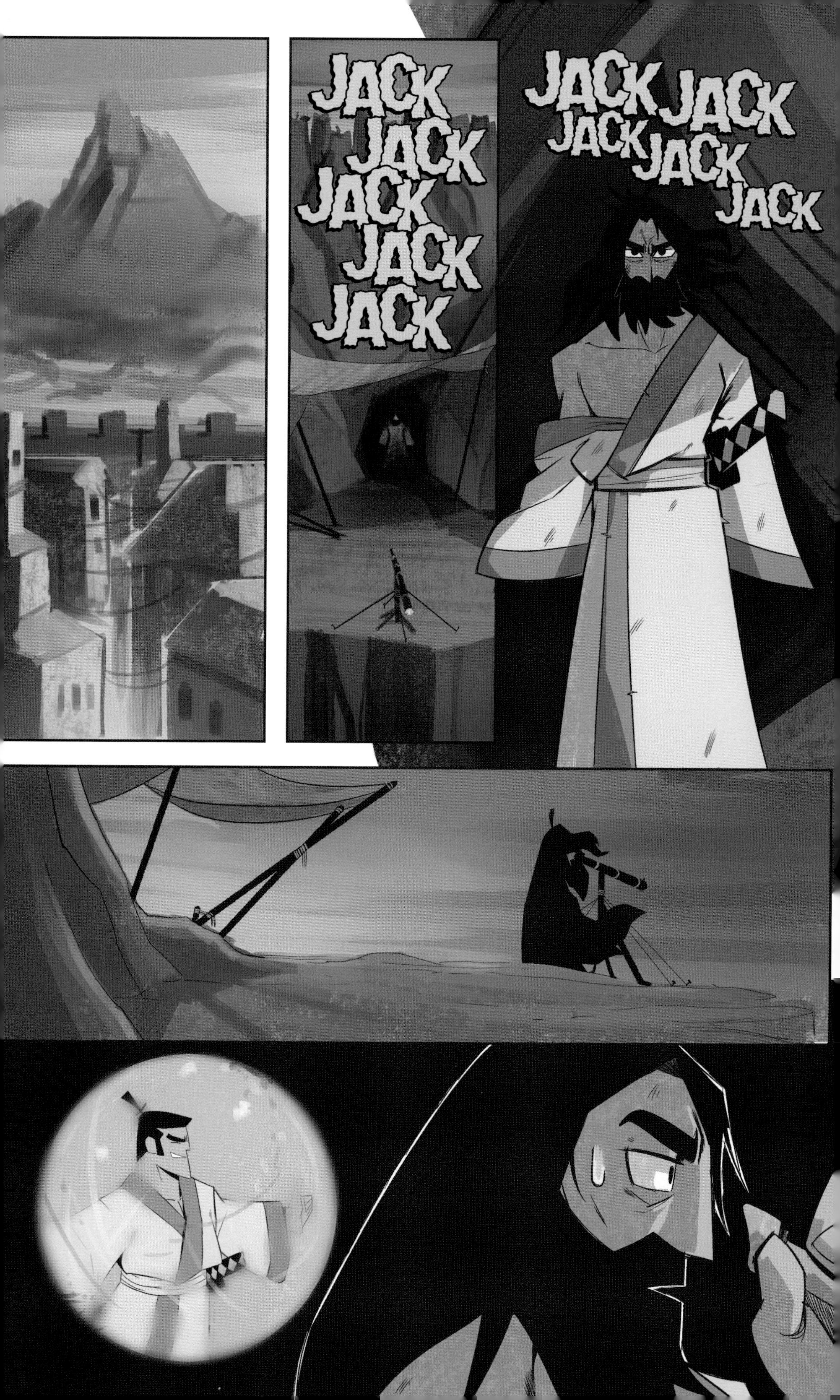
JACK
JACK
JACK
JACK
JACK
JACK JACK
JACK JACK
JACK

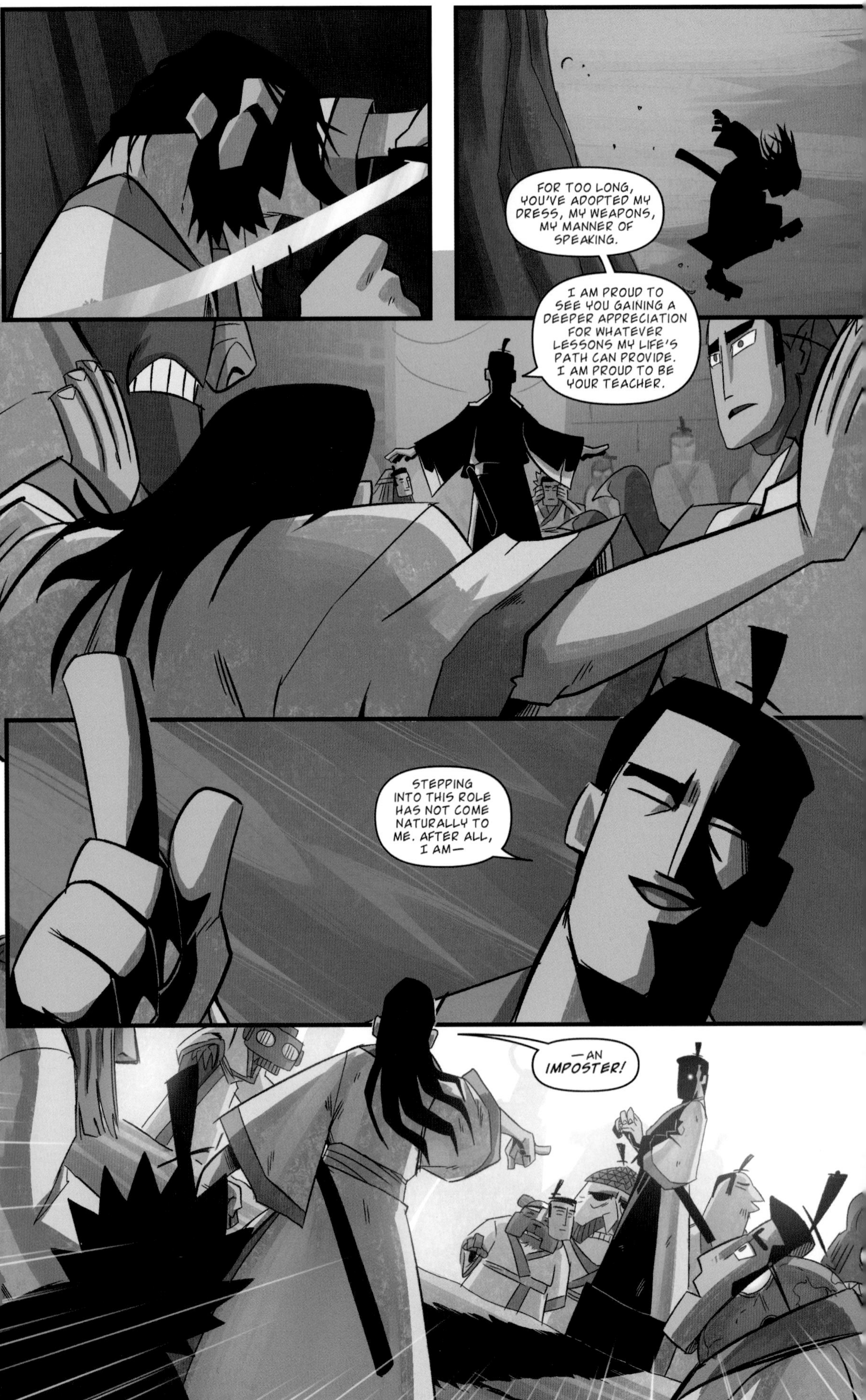
FOR TOO LONG, YOU'VE ADOPTED MY DRESS, MY WEAPONS, MY MANNER OF SPEAKING.
I AM PROUD TO SEE YOU GAINING A DEEPER APPRECIATION FOR WHATEVER LESSONS MY LIFE'S PATH CAN PROVIDE. I AM PROUD TO BE YOUR TEACHER.
STEPPING INTO THIS ROLE HAS NOT COME NATURALLY TO ME. AFTER ALL, I AM—
—AN *IMPOSTER!*

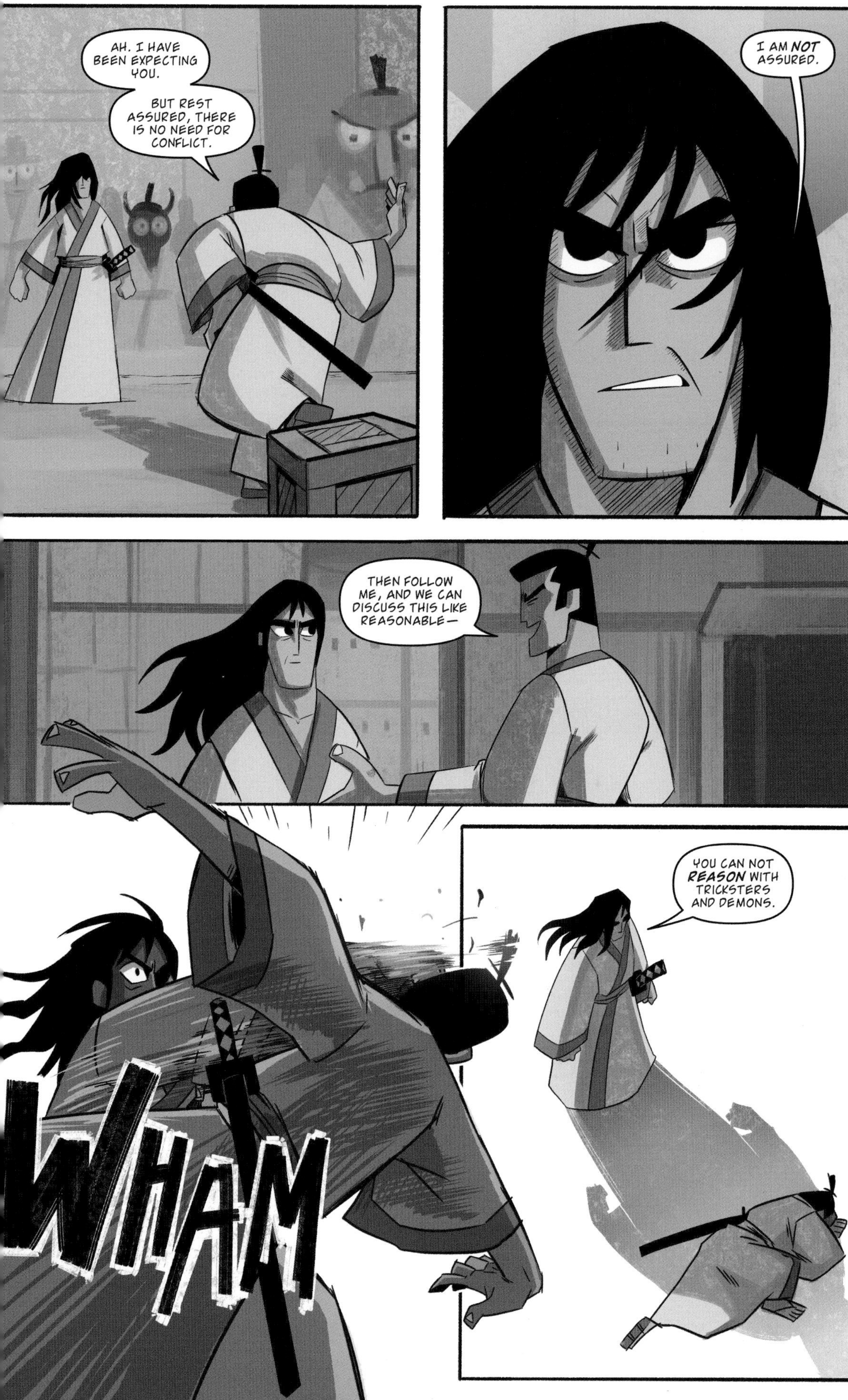
AH. I HAVE BEEN EXPECTING YOU.
BUT REST ASSURED, THERE IS NO NEED FOR CONFLICT.
I AM NOT ASSURED.
THEN FOLLOW ME, AND WE CAN DISCUSS THIS LIKE REASONABLE—
WHAM
YOU CAN NOT REASON WITH TRICKSTERS AND DEMONS.

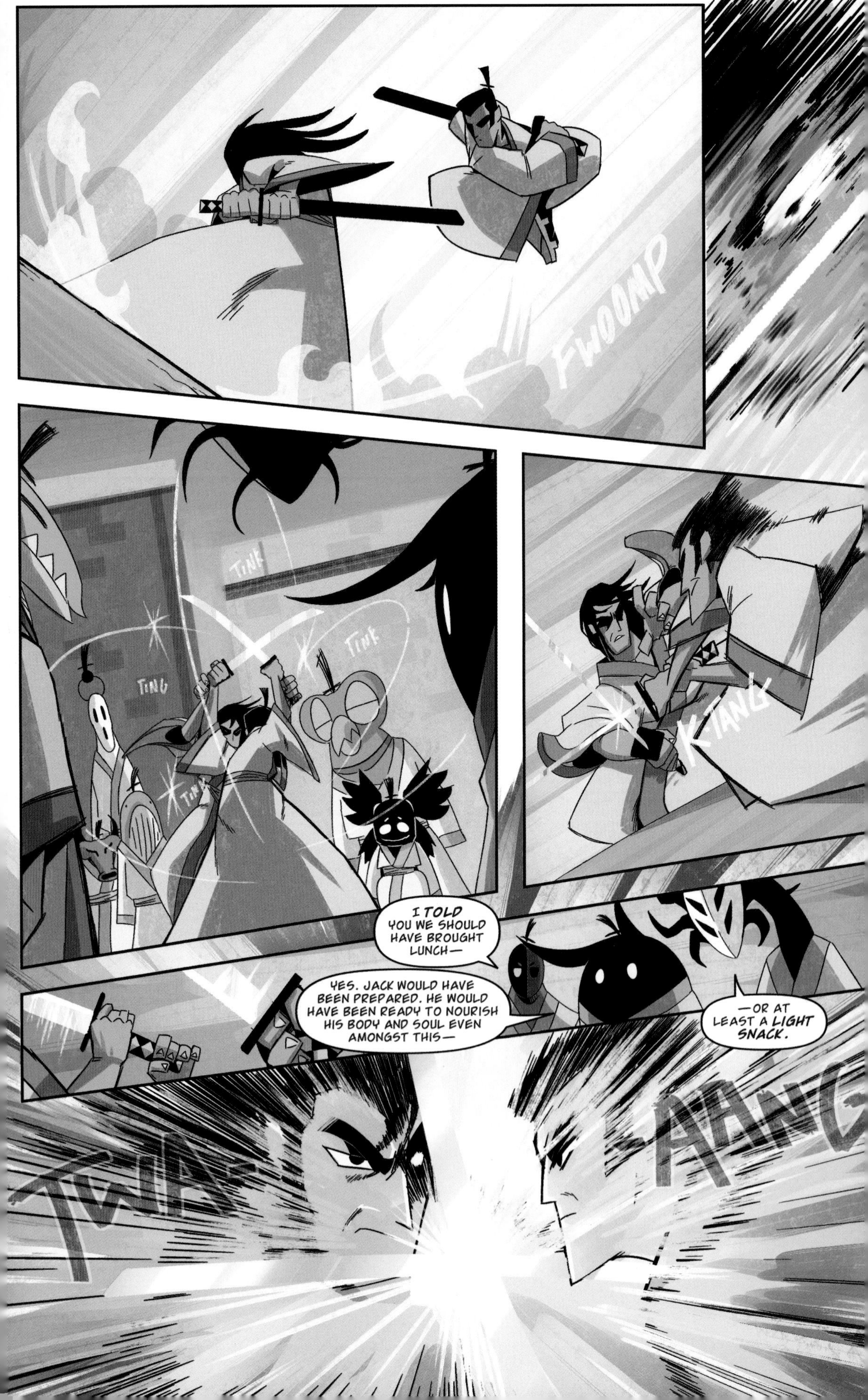
FWOOMP
TINK
TINK
TING
TINK
K-TANG
I TOLD YOU WE SHOULD HAVE BROUGHT LUNCH—
YES. JACK WOULD HAVE BEEN PREPARED. HE WOULD HAVE BEEN READY TO NOURISH HIS BODY AND SOUL EVEN AMONGST THIS—
—OR AT LEAST A LIGHT SNACK.
ANG

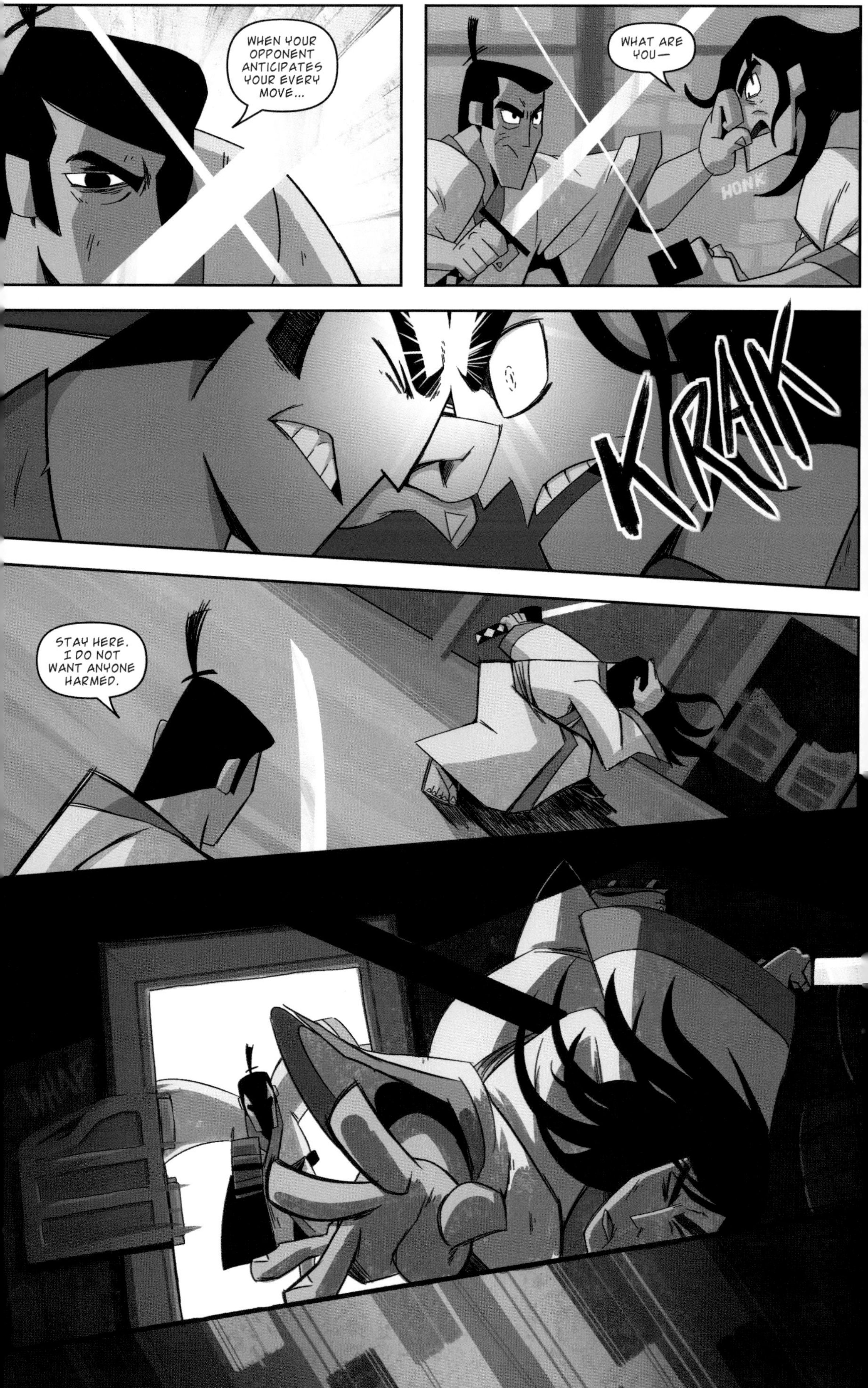
WHEN YOUR OPPONENT ANTICIPATES YOUR EVERY MOVE...
WHAT ARE YOU—
HONK
KRAK
STAY HERE. I DO NOT WANT ANYONE HARMED.

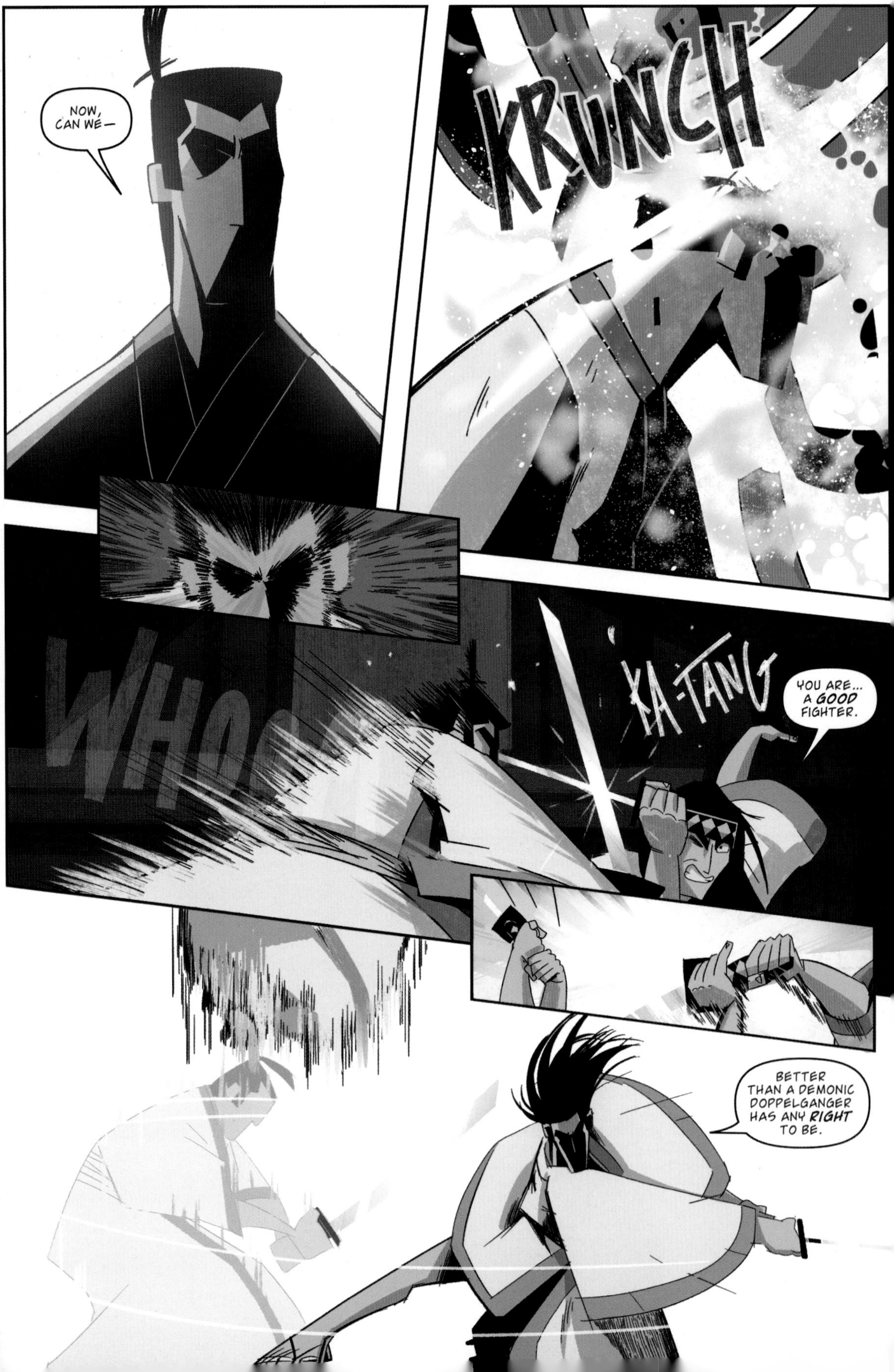
NOW, CAN WE—
KRUNCH
XA-TANG
YOU ARE... A GOOD FIGHTER.
BETTER THAN A DEMONIC DOPPELGANGER HAS ANY RIGHT TO BE.

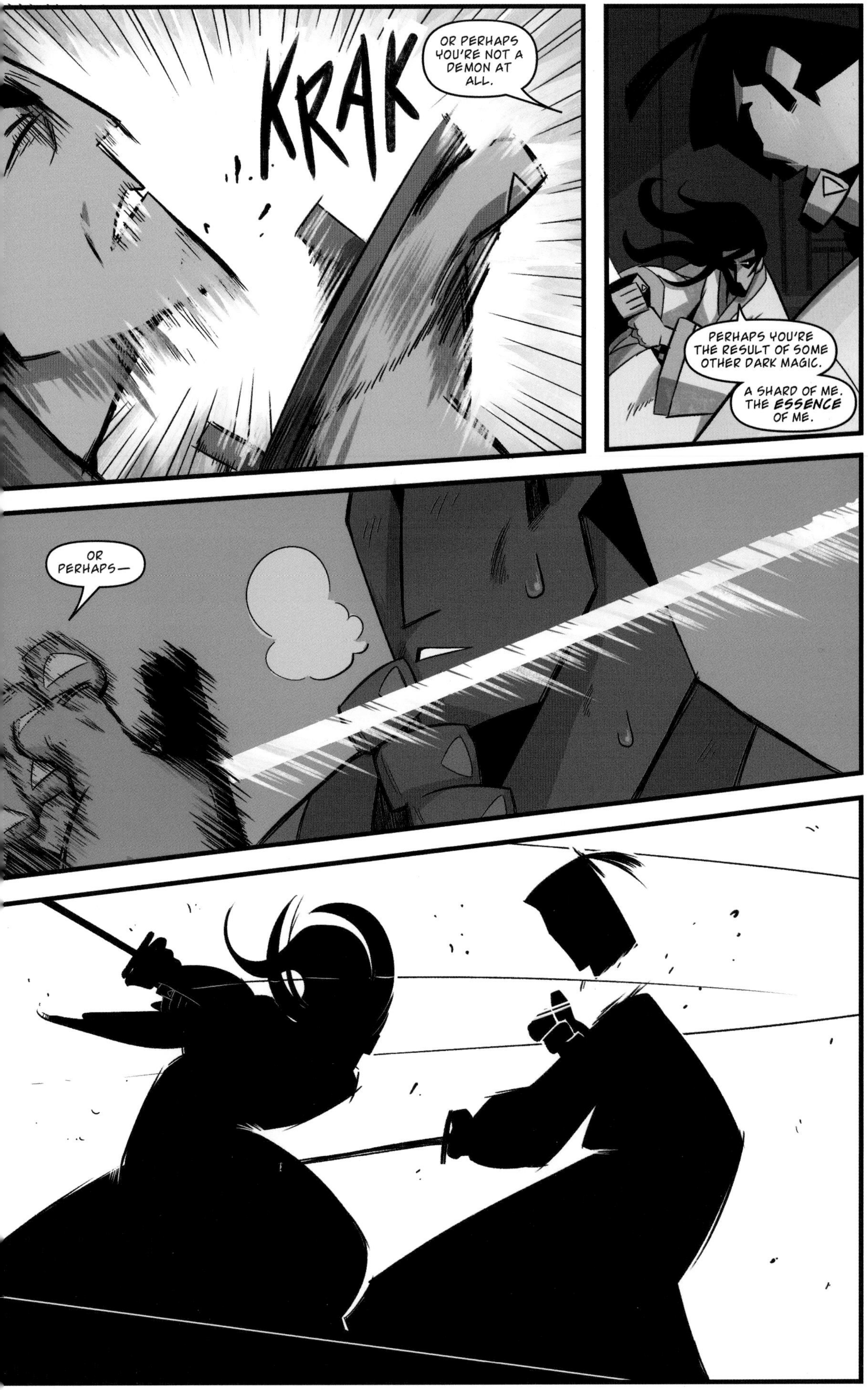
KRAK
OR PERHAPS YOU'RE NOT A DEMON AT ALL.
PERHAPS YOU'RE THE RESULT OF SOME OTHER DARK MAGIC.
A SHARD OF ME. THE ESSENCE OF ME.
OR PERHAPS—

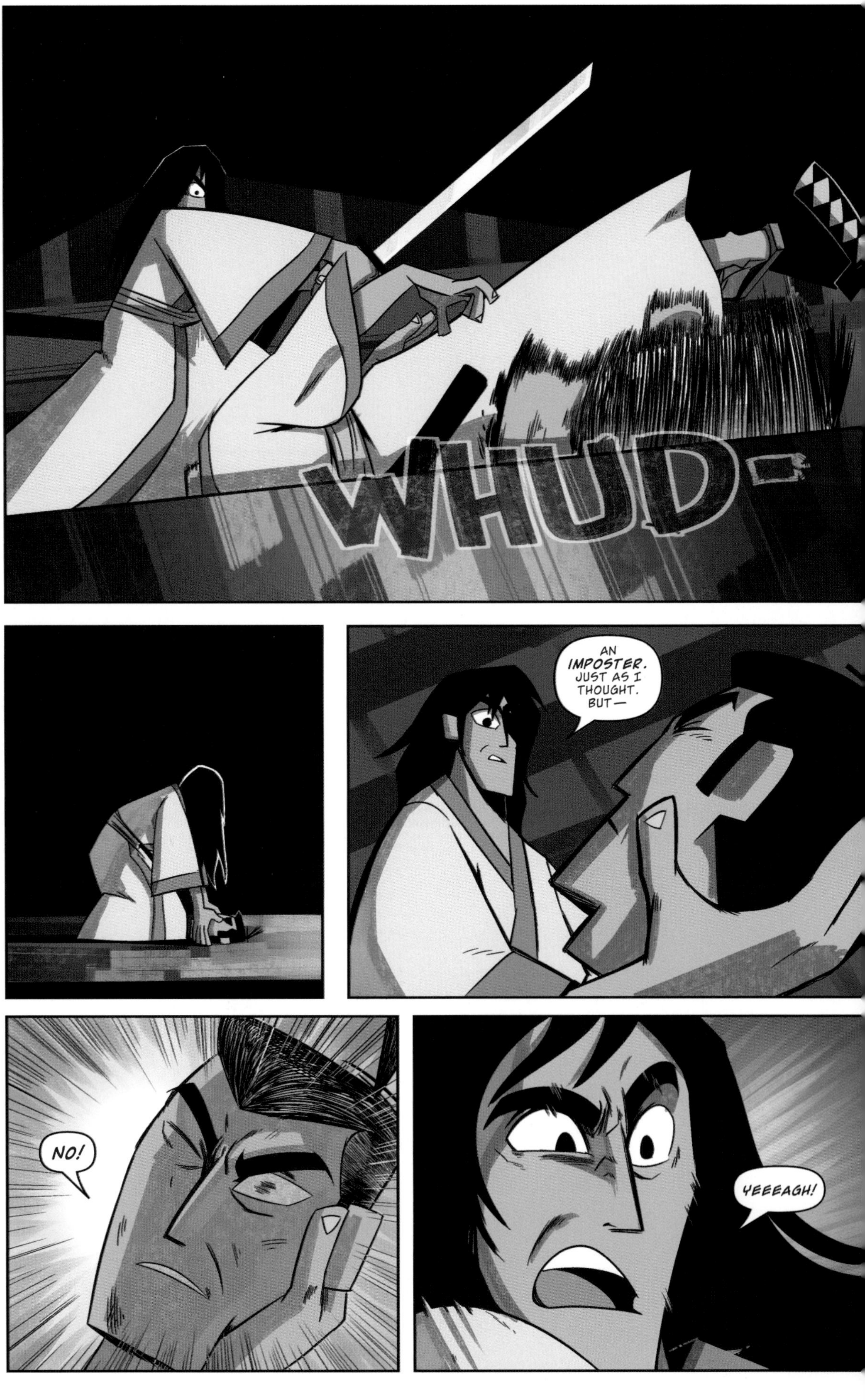
WHUD
AN IMPOSTER. JUST AS I THOUGHT. BUT—
NO!
YEEEAGH!

A ROBOT, YES. BUT NOT AN **IMPOSTER**.

"THE PEOPLE OF THIS VILLAGE WANTED TO FOLLOW IN YOUR FOOTSTEPS. BUT THEY DID NOT KNOW **HOW**.

"A GROUP OF SCIENTISTS—FUNDAMENTALISTS—SAW THAT OUR SOCIETY WAS DRIFTING IN THE WRONG DIRECTION.

JAK V.01

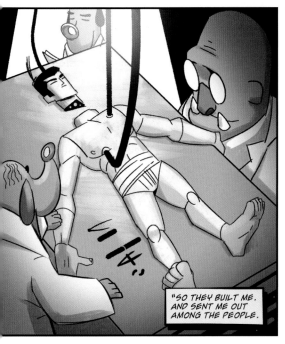

"SO THEY BUILT ME. AND SENT ME OUT AMONG THE PEOPLE.

"AT FIRST, IT DID NOT GO WELL. THEY IGNORED ME. ASSUMED I WAS AN IMPOSTER. THEY LISTENED BUT DID NOT HEAR."

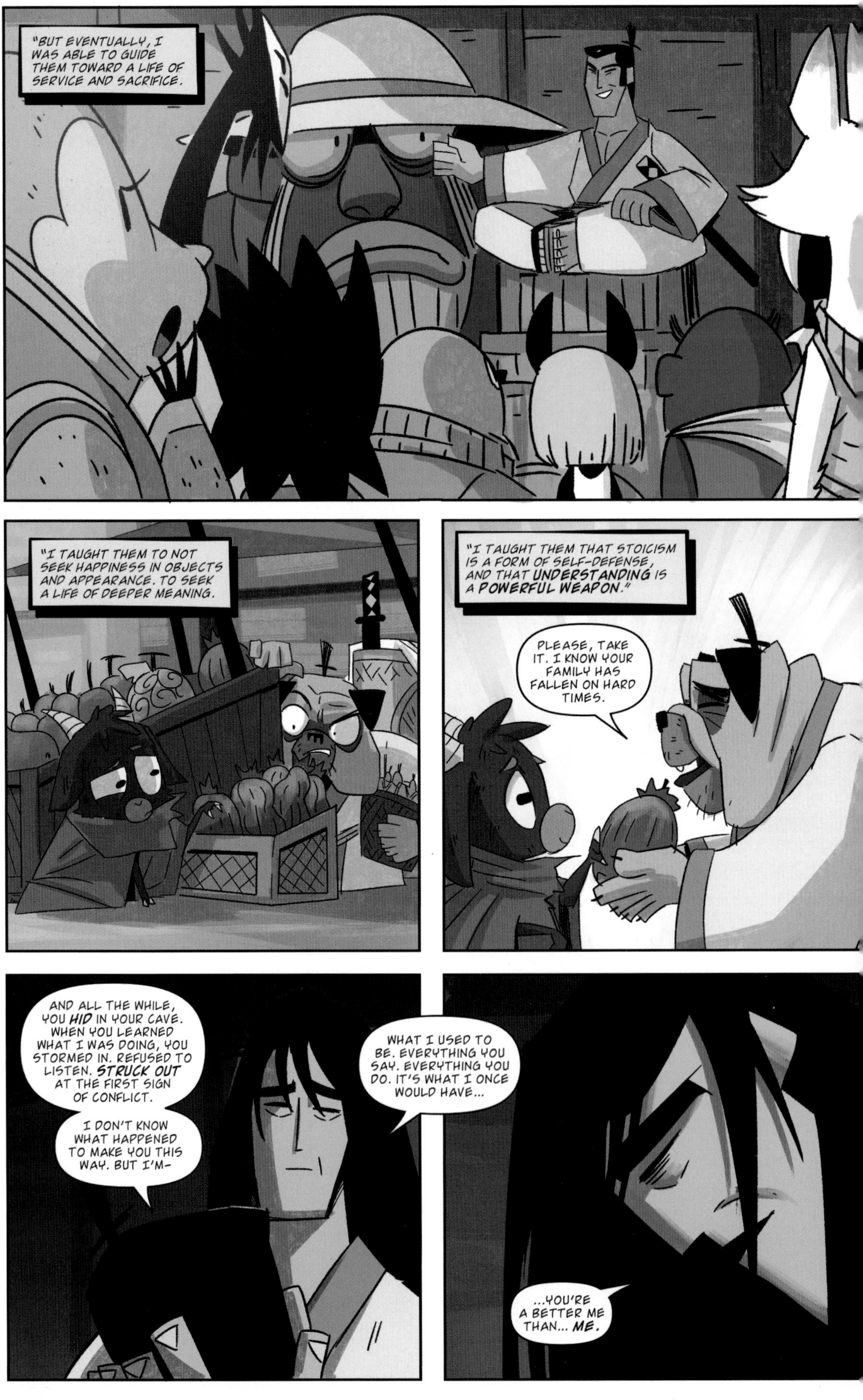
"BUT EVENTUALLY, I WAS ABLE TO GUIDE THEM TOWARD A LIFE OF SERVICE AND SACRIFICE.
"I TAUGHT THEM TO NOT SEEK HAPPINESS IN OBJECTS AND APPEARANCE. TO SEEK A LIFE OF DEEPER MEANING.
"I TAUGHT THEM THAT STOICISM IS A FORM OF SELF-DEFENSE, AND THAT UNDERSTANDING IS A POWERFUL WEAPON."
PLEASE, TAKE IT. I KNOW YOUR FAMILY HAS FALLEN ON HARD TIMES.
AND ALL THE WHILE, YOU HID IN YOUR CAVE. WHEN YOU LEARNED WHAT I WAS DOING, YOU STORMED IN. REFUSED TO LISTEN. STRUCK OUT AT THE FIRST SIGN OF CONFLICT.
I DON'T KNOW WHAT HAPPENED TO MAKE YOU THIS WAY. BUT I'M-
WHAT I USED TO BE. EVERYTHING YOU SAY. EVERYTHING YOU DO. IT'S WHAT I ONCE WOULD HAVE...
...YOU'RE A BETTER ME THAN... ME.

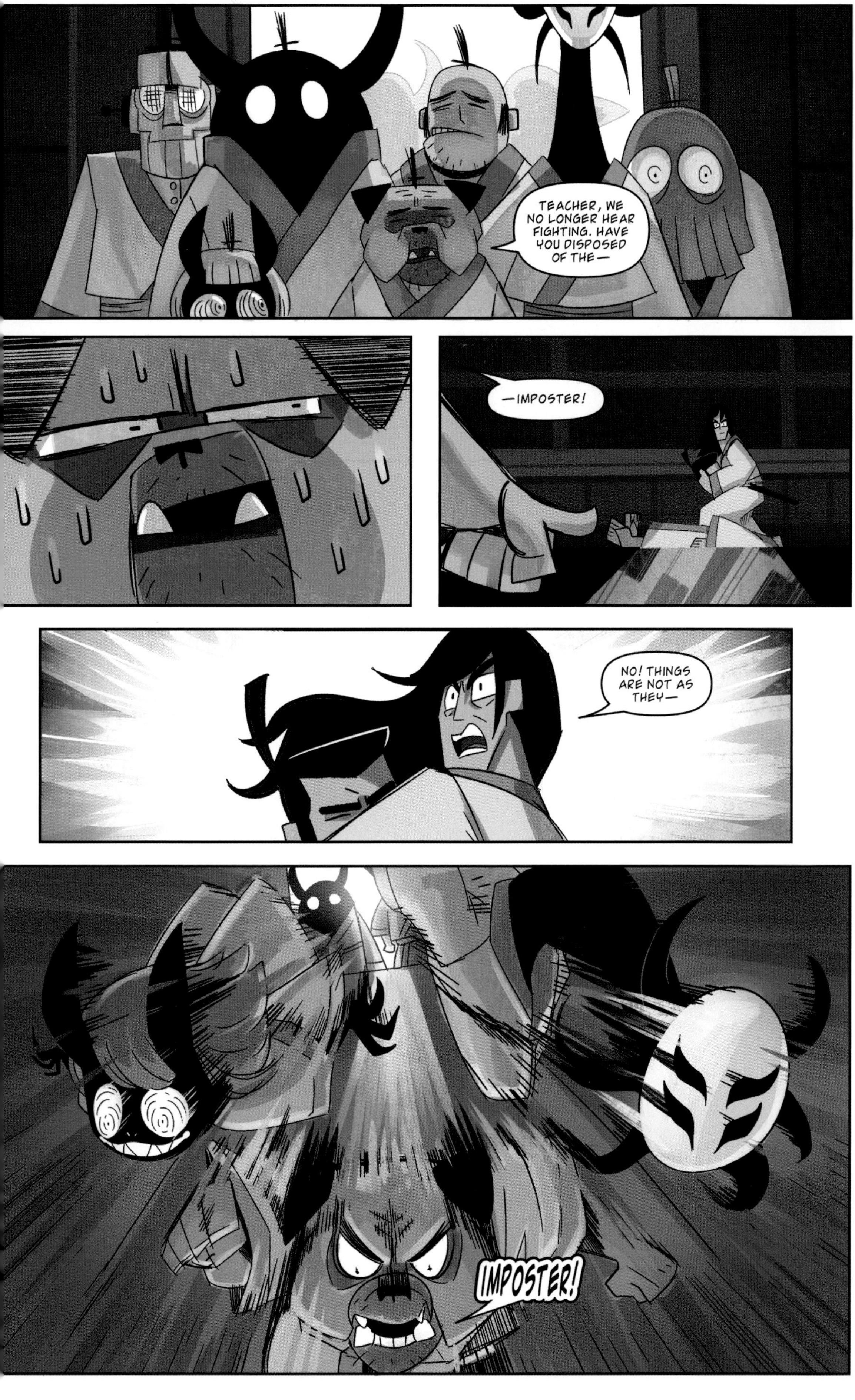
TEACHER, WE NO LONGER HEAR FIGHTING. HAVE YOU DISPOSED OF THE—
—IMPOSTER!
NO! THINGS ARE NOT AS THEY—
IMPOSTER!

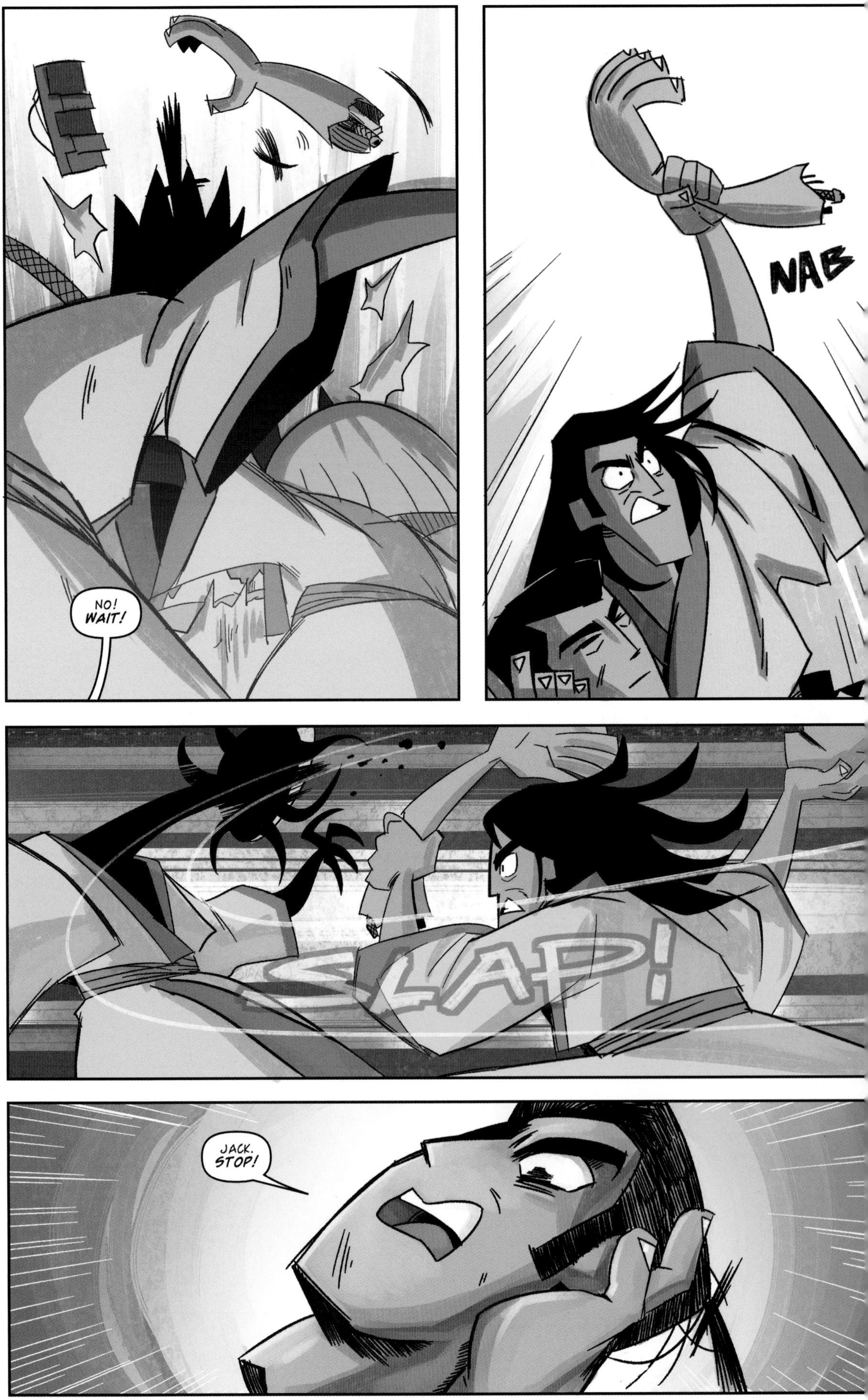
NO!
WAIT!
NAB
SLAP!
JACK.
STOP!

YOU WERE WRONG. THESE PEOPLE DO *NOT* FOLLOW MY WAYS.

THEY WANT TO.

THERE IS NO POINT IN FIGHTING THEM. THEY FEEL SCARED AND—

ZZZZZZZZZZZ

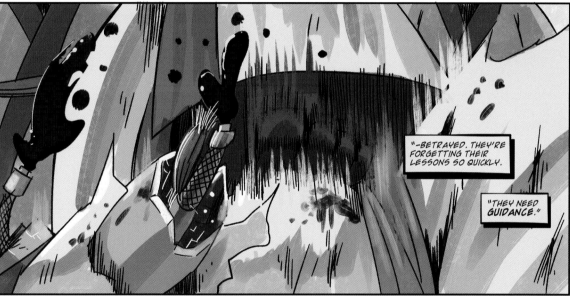

"—BETRAYED. THEY'RE FORGETTING THEIR LESSONS SO QUICKLY."

"THEY NEED *GUIDANCE.*"

THEY NEED SOMEONE TO—

ZZZZZZZZZZZZ

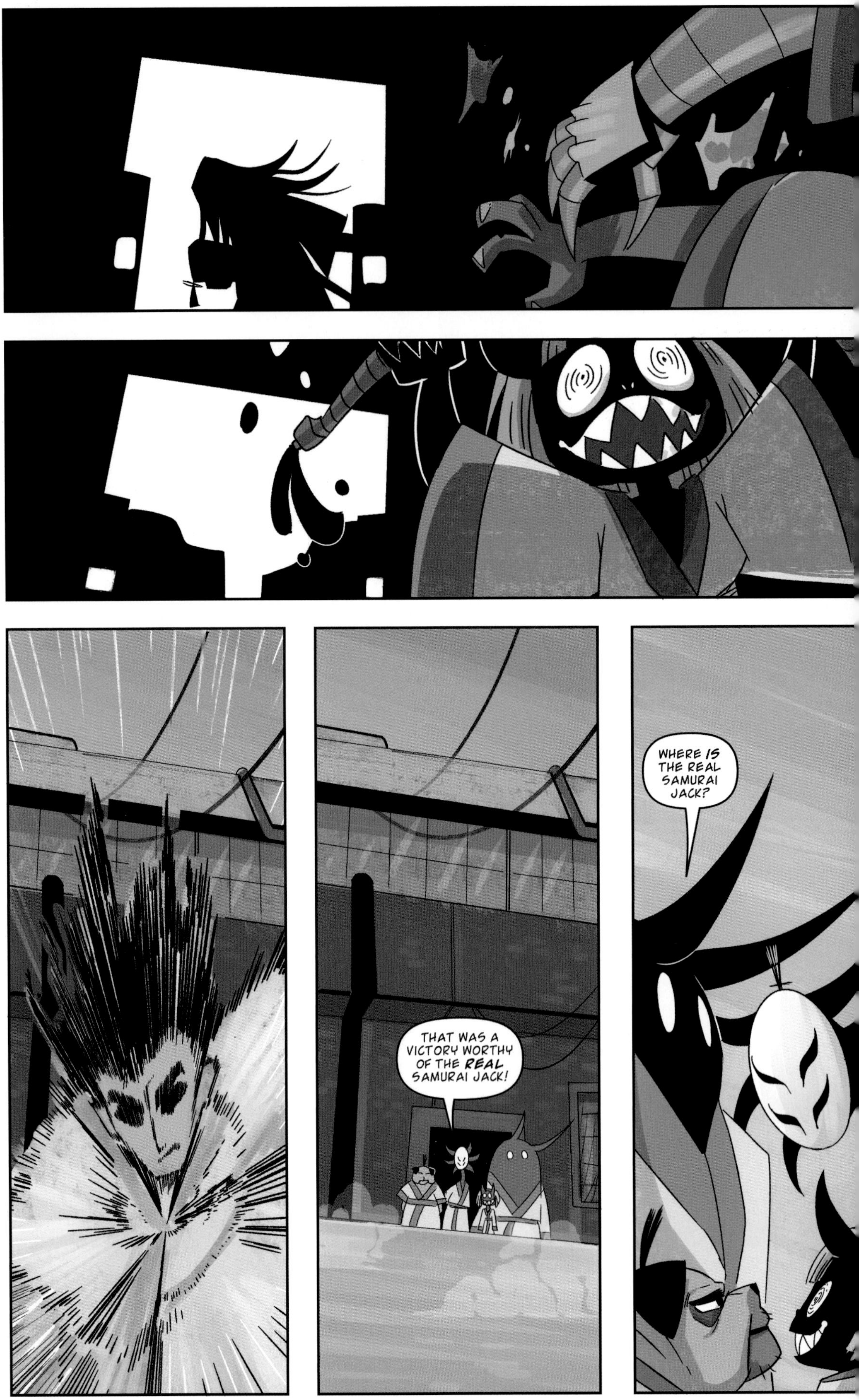
THAT WAS A VICTORY WORTHY OF THE REAL SAMURAI JACK!
WHERE IS THE REAL SAMURAI JACK?

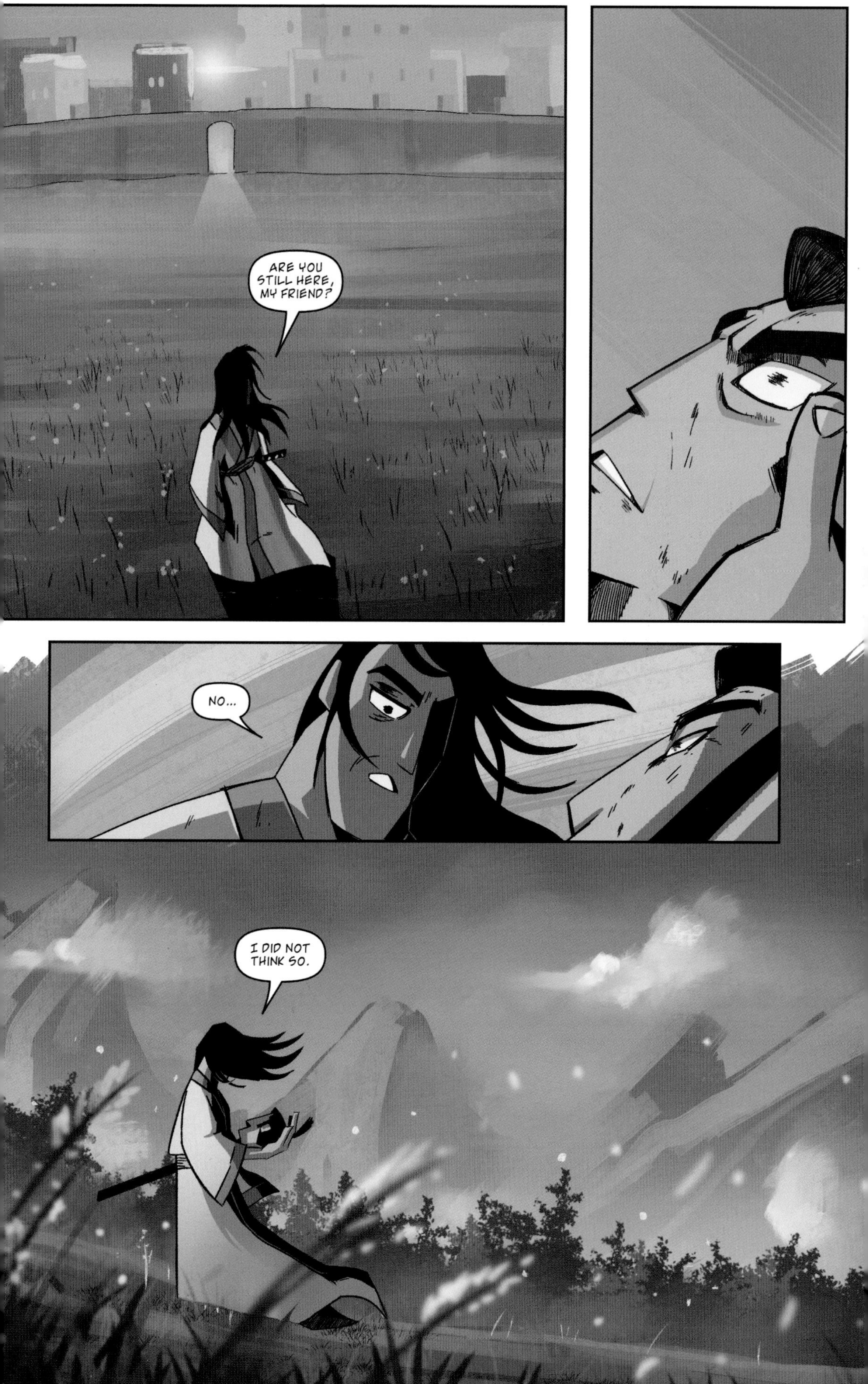
ARE YOU STILL HERE, MY FRIEND?
NO...
I DID NOT THINK SO.

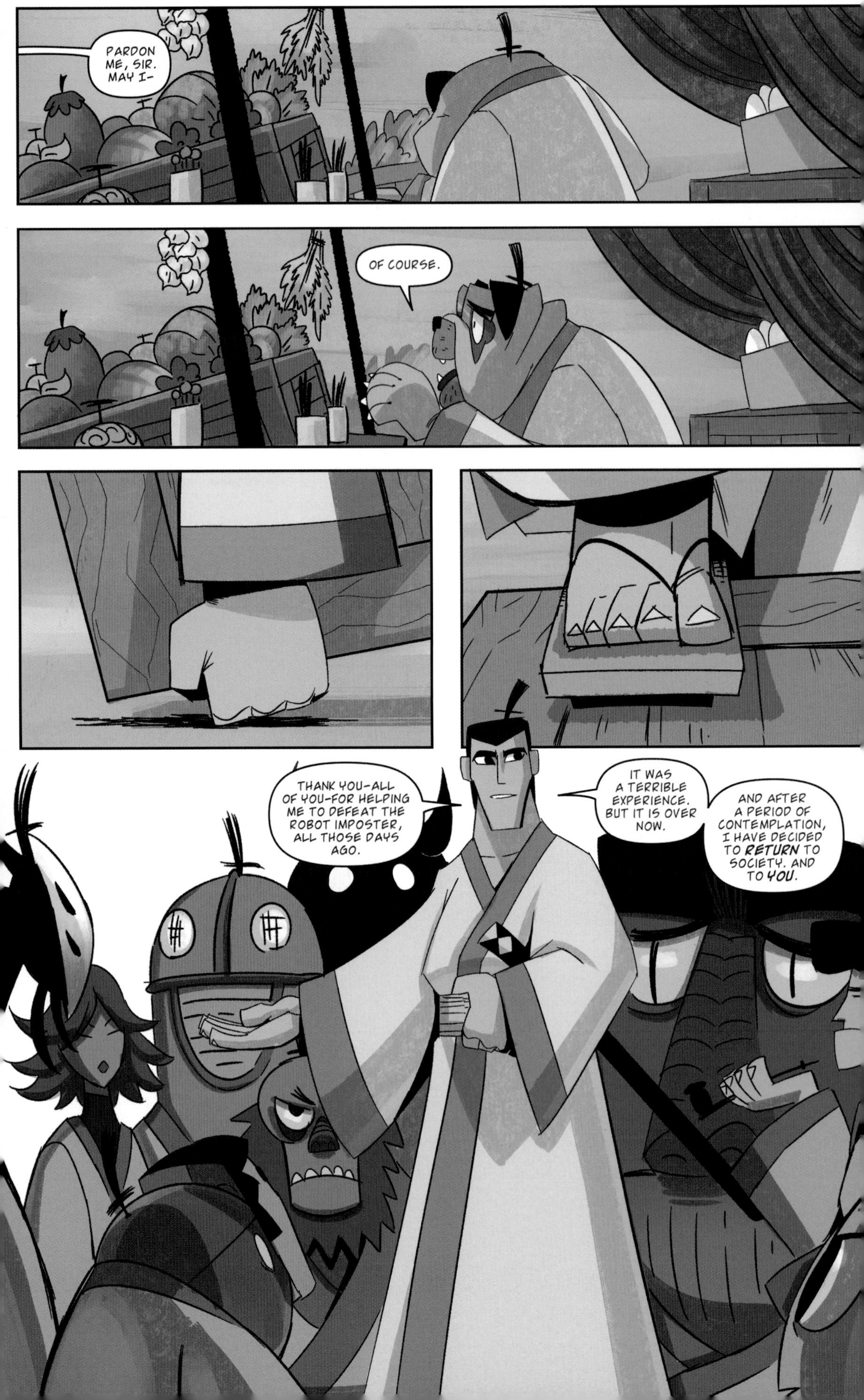
PARDON ME, SIR. MAY I-
OF COURSE.
THANK YOU-ALL OF YOU-FOR HELPING ME TO DEFEAT THE ROBOT IMPOSTER, ALL THOSE DAYS AGO.
IT WAS A TERRIBLE EXPERIENCE. BUT IT IS OVER NOW.
AND AFTER A PERIOD OF CONTEMPLATION, I HAVE DECIDED TO RETURN TO SOCIETY. AND TO YOU.

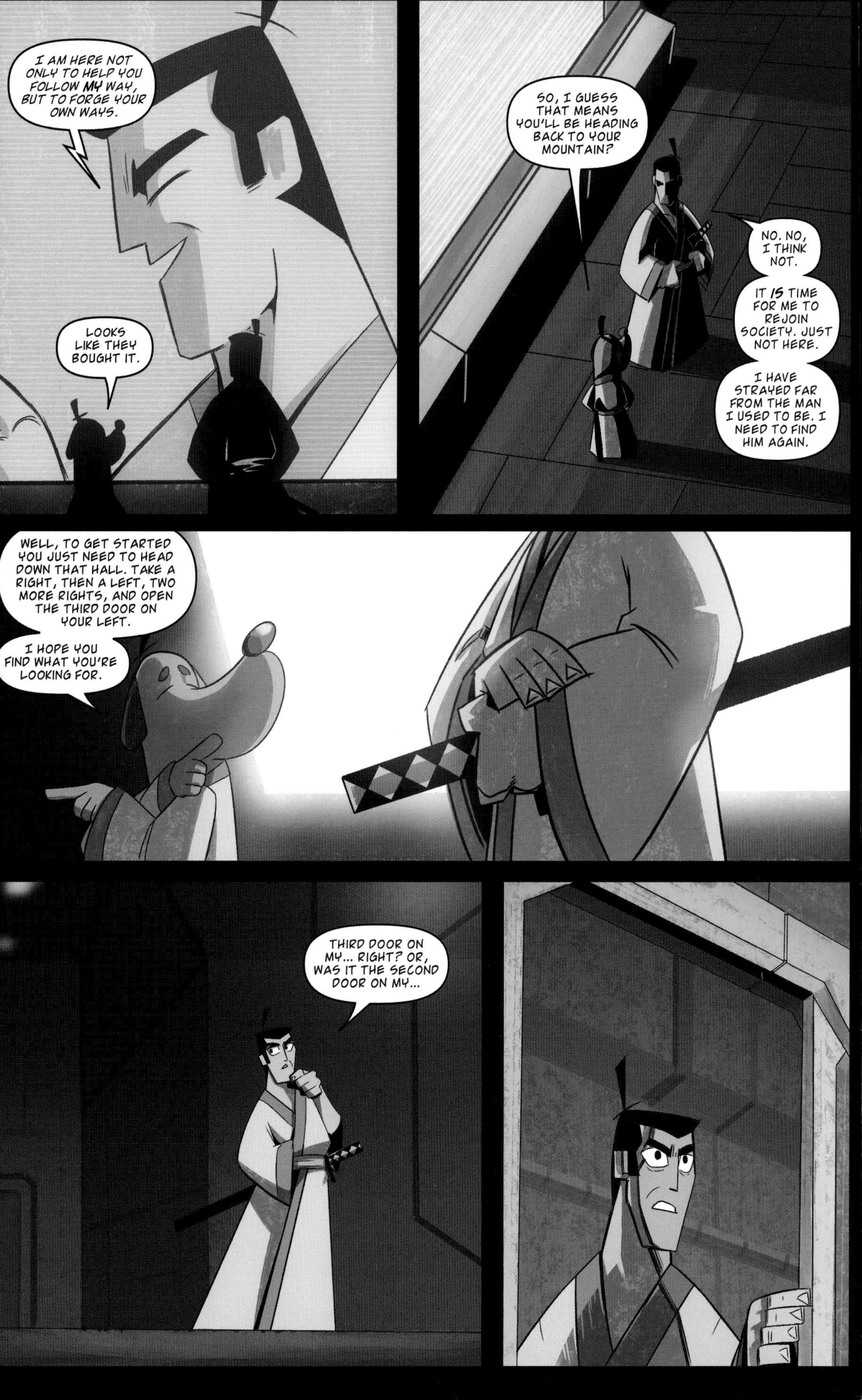
I AM HERE NOT ONLY TO HELP YOU FOLLOW MY WAY, BUT TO FORGE YOUR OWN WAYS.
LOOKS LIKE THEY BOUGHT IT.
SO, I GUESS THAT MEANS YOU'LL BE HEADING BACK TO YOUR MOUNTAIN?
NO. NO, I THINK NOT.
IT IS TIME FOR ME TO REJOIN SOCIETY. JUST NOT HERE.
I HAVE STRAYED FAR FROM THE MAN I USED TO BE. I NEED TO FIND HIM AGAIN.
WELL, TO GET STARTED YOU JUST NEED TO HEAD DOWN THAT HALL. TAKE A RIGHT, THEN A LEFT, TWO MORE RIGHTS, AND OPEN THE THIRD DOOR ON YOUR LEFT.
I HOPE YOU FIND WHAT YOU'RE LOOKING FOR.
THIRD DOOR ON MY... RIGHT? OR, WAS IT THE SECOND DOOR ON MY...

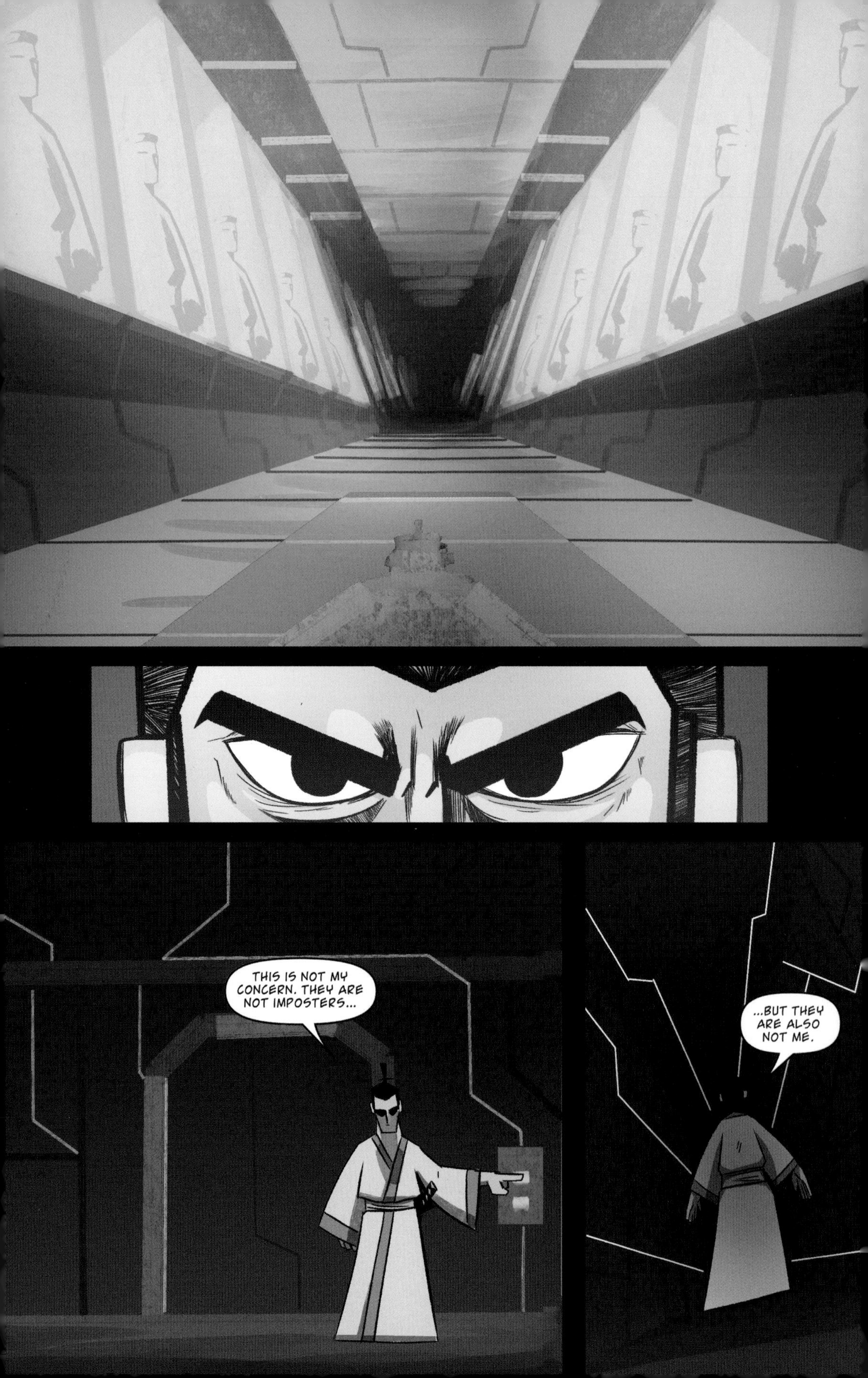
THIS IS NOT MY CONCERN. THEY ARE NOT IMPOSTERS...
...BUT THEY ARE ALSO NOT ME.

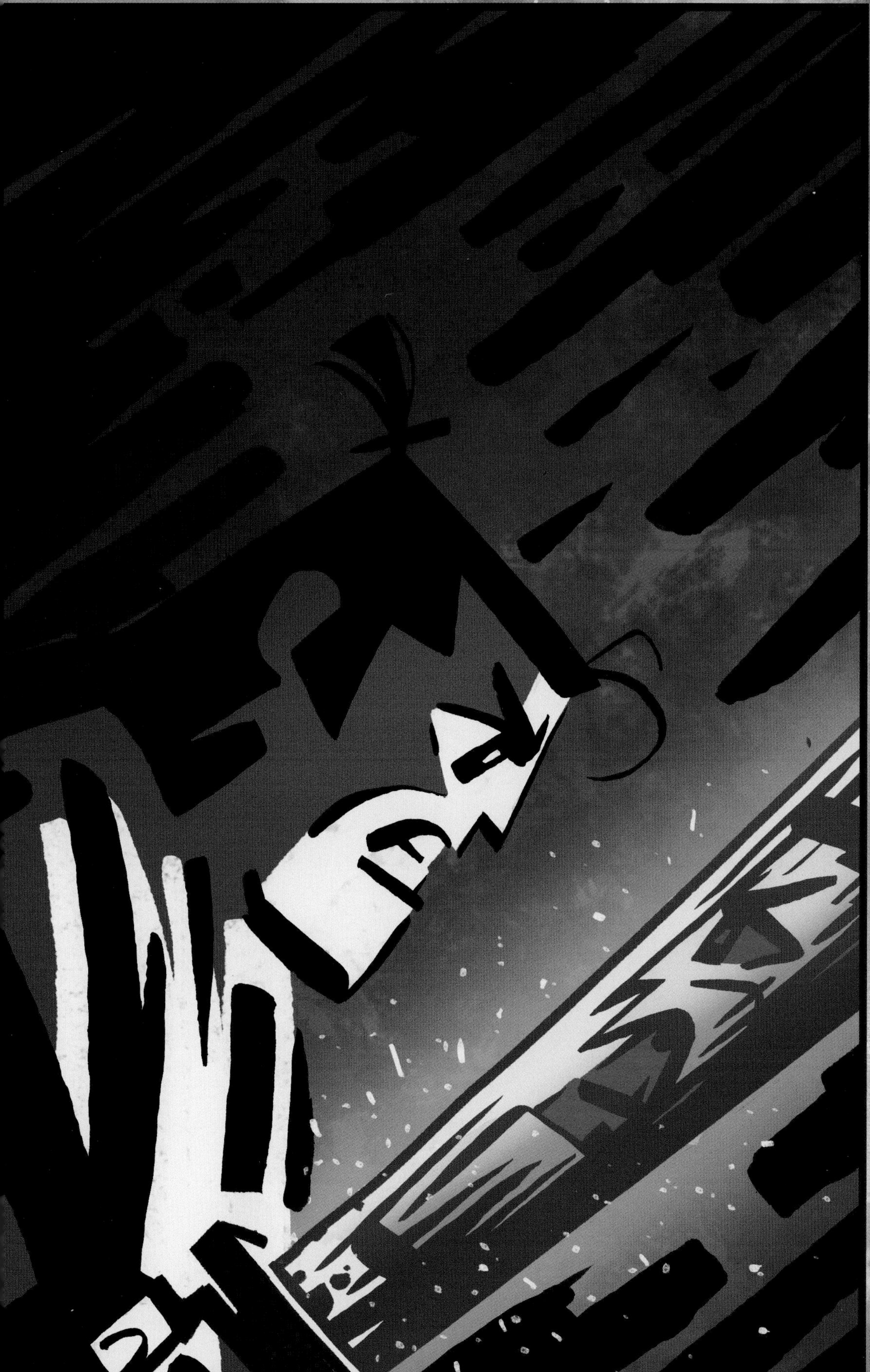
Art by Gavin Fullerton

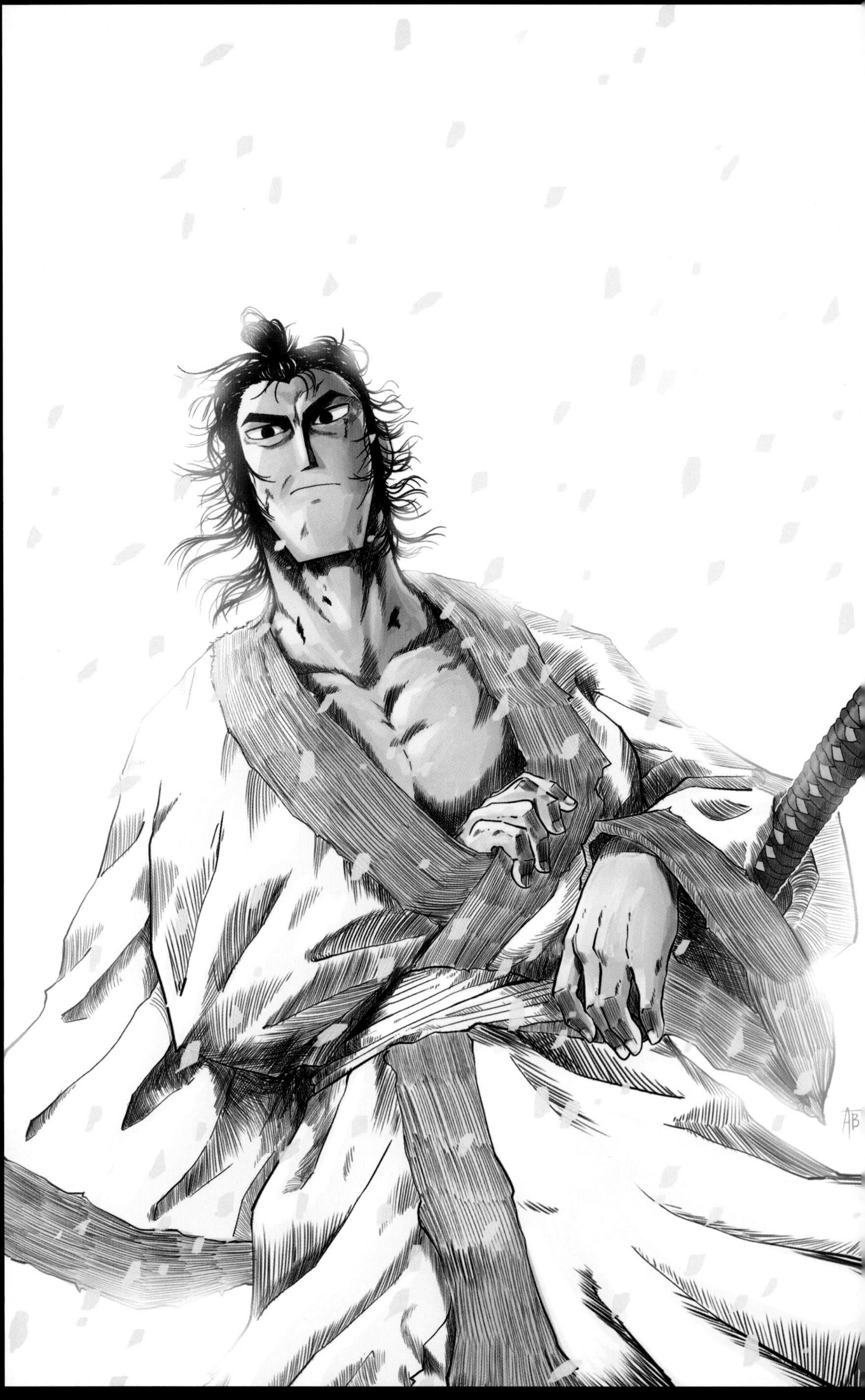
AB

Art by Adam Bryce Thomas

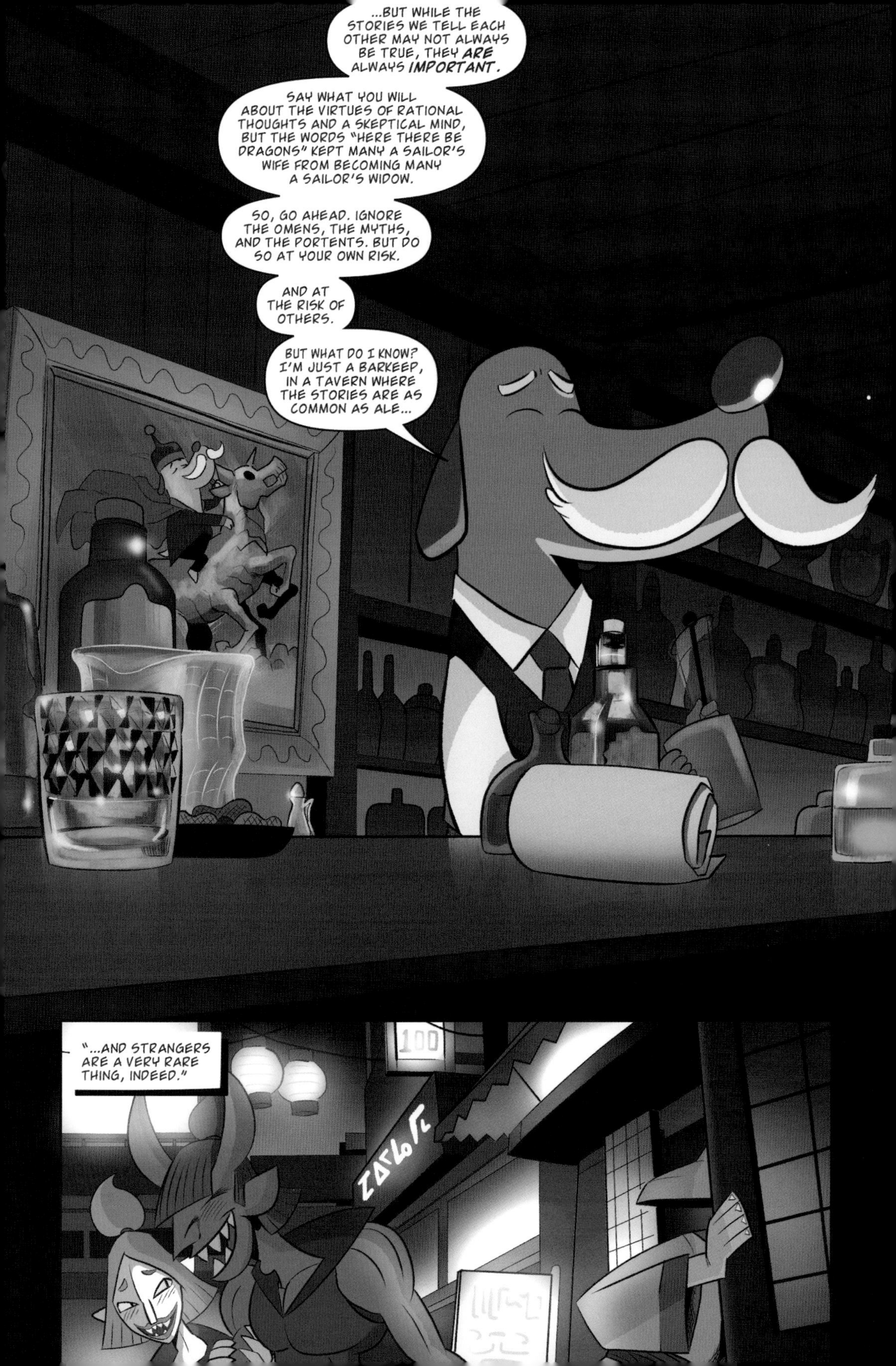

...BUT WHILE THE STORIES WE TELL EACH OTHER MAY NOT ALWAYS BE TRUE, THEY **ARE** ALWAYS **IMPORTANT**.
SAY WHAT YOU WILL ABOUT THE VIRTUES OF RATIONAL THOUGHTS AND A SKEPTICAL MIND, BUT THE WORDS "HERE THERE BE DRAGONS" KEPT MANY A SAILOR'S WIFE FROM BECOMING MANY A SAILOR'S WIDOW.
SO, GO AHEAD. IGNORE THE OMENS, THE MYTHS, AND THE PORTENTS. BUT DO SO AT YOUR OWN RISK.
AND AT THE RISK OF OTHERS.
BUT WHAT DO I KNOW? I'M JUST A BARKEEP, IN A TAVERN WHERE THE STORIES ARE AS COMMON AS ALE...
"...AND STRANGERS ARE A VERY RARE THING, INDEED."
100

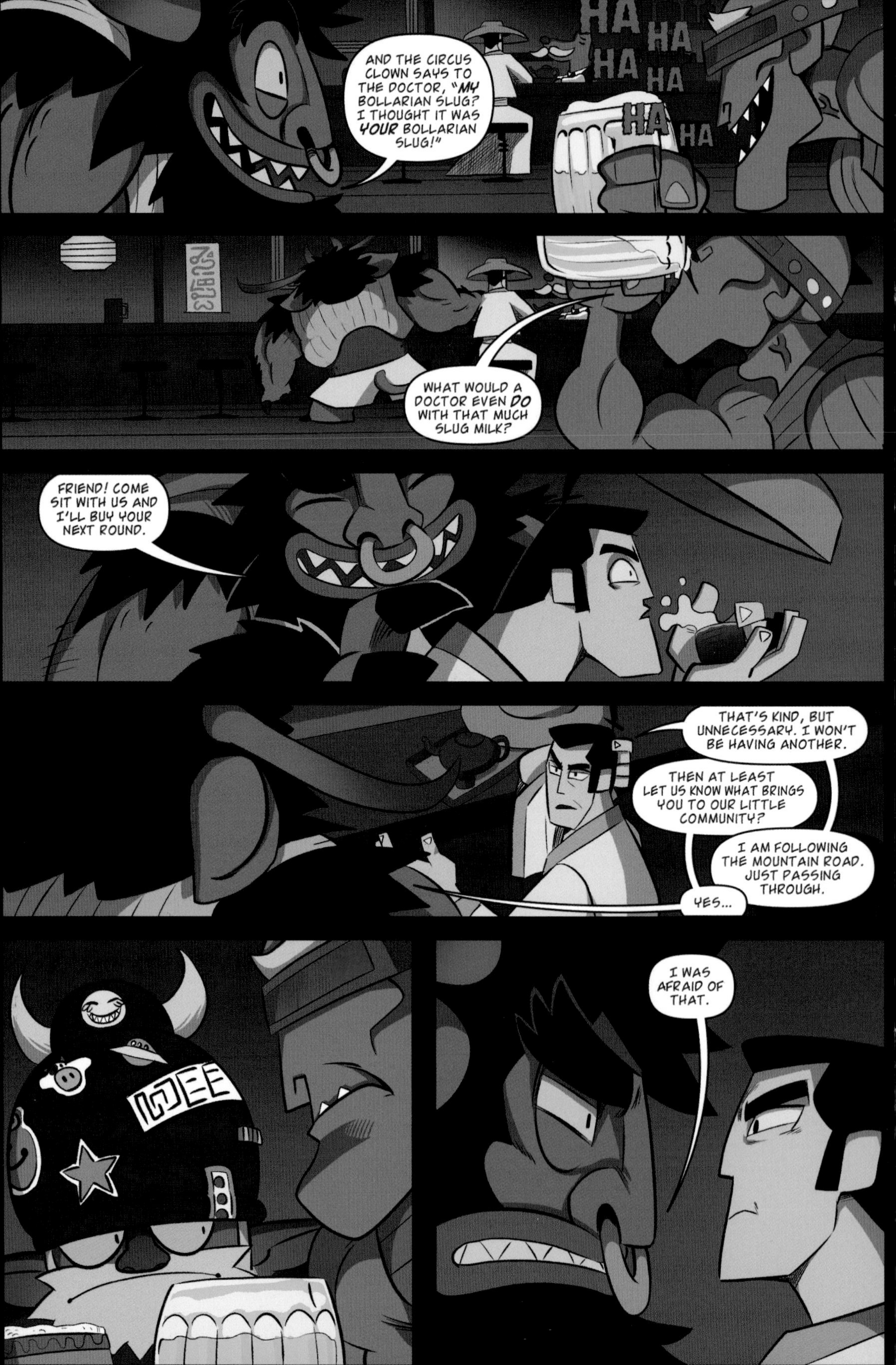
HA HA HA HA HA HA
AND THE CIRCUS CLOWN SAYS TO THE DOCTOR, "MY BOLLARIAN SLUG? I THOUGHT IT WAS YOUR BOLLARIAN SLUG!"
WHAT WOULD A DOCTOR EVEN DO WITH THAT MUCH SLUG MILK?
FRIEND! COME SIT WITH US AND I'LL BUY YOUR NEXT ROUND.
THAT'S KIND, BUT UNNECESSARY. I WON'T BE HAVING ANOTHER.
THEN AT LEAST LET US KNOW WHAT BRINGS YOU TO OUR LITTLE COMMUNITY?
I AM FOLLOWING THE MOUNTAIN ROAD. JUST PASSING THROUGH.
YES...
WEE
I WAS AFRAID OF THAT.

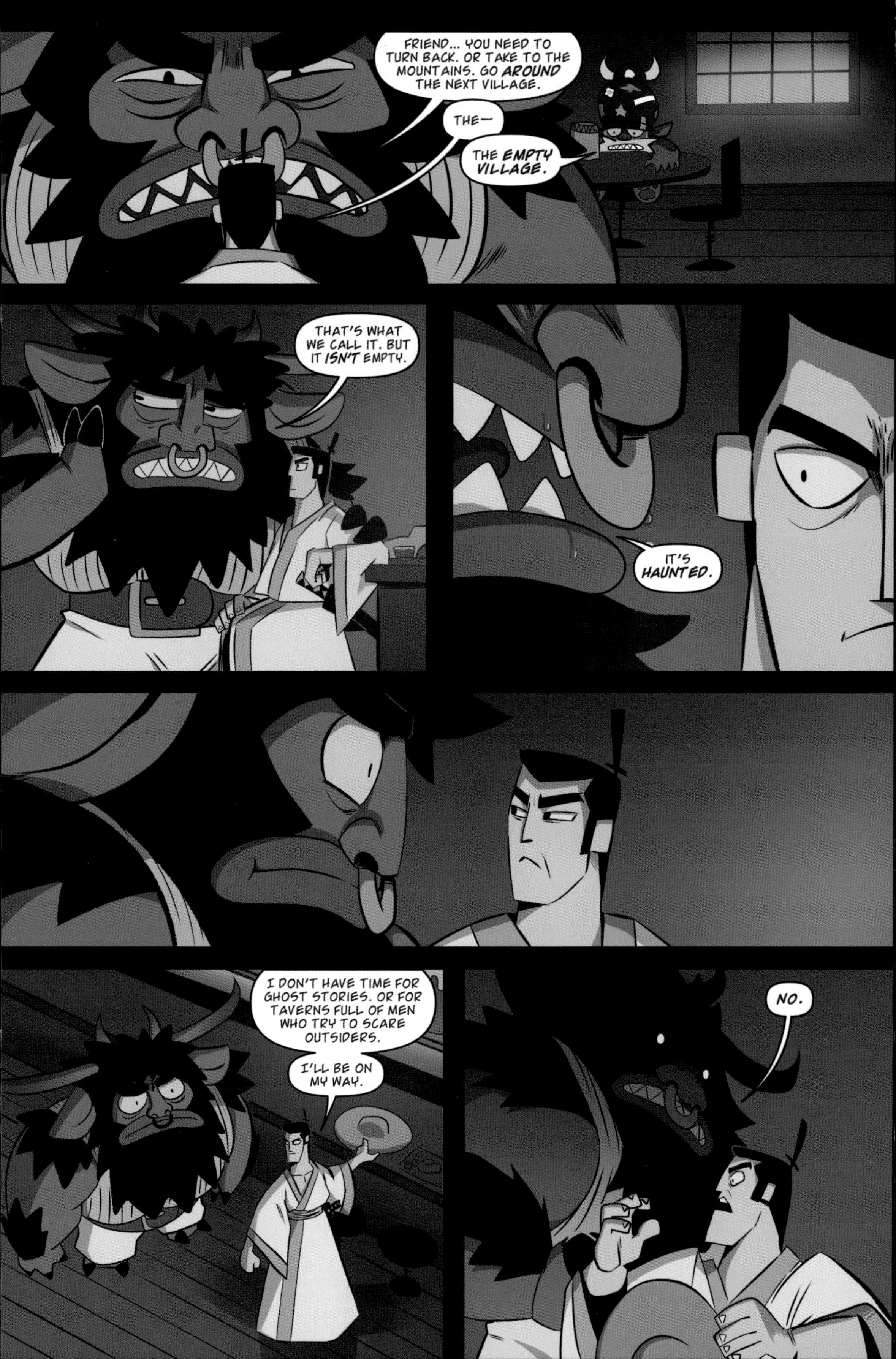
FRIEND... YOU NEED TO TURN BACK. OR TAKE TO THE MOUNTAINS. GO AROUND THE NEXT VILLAGE.
THE—
THE EMPTY VILLAGE.
THAT'S WHAT WE CALL IT. BUT IT ISN'T EMPTY.
IT'S HAUNTED.
I DON'T HAVE TIME FOR GHOST STORIES. OR FOR TAVERNS FULL OF MEN WHO TRY TO SCARE OUTSIDERS.
I'LL BE ON MY WAY.
NO.

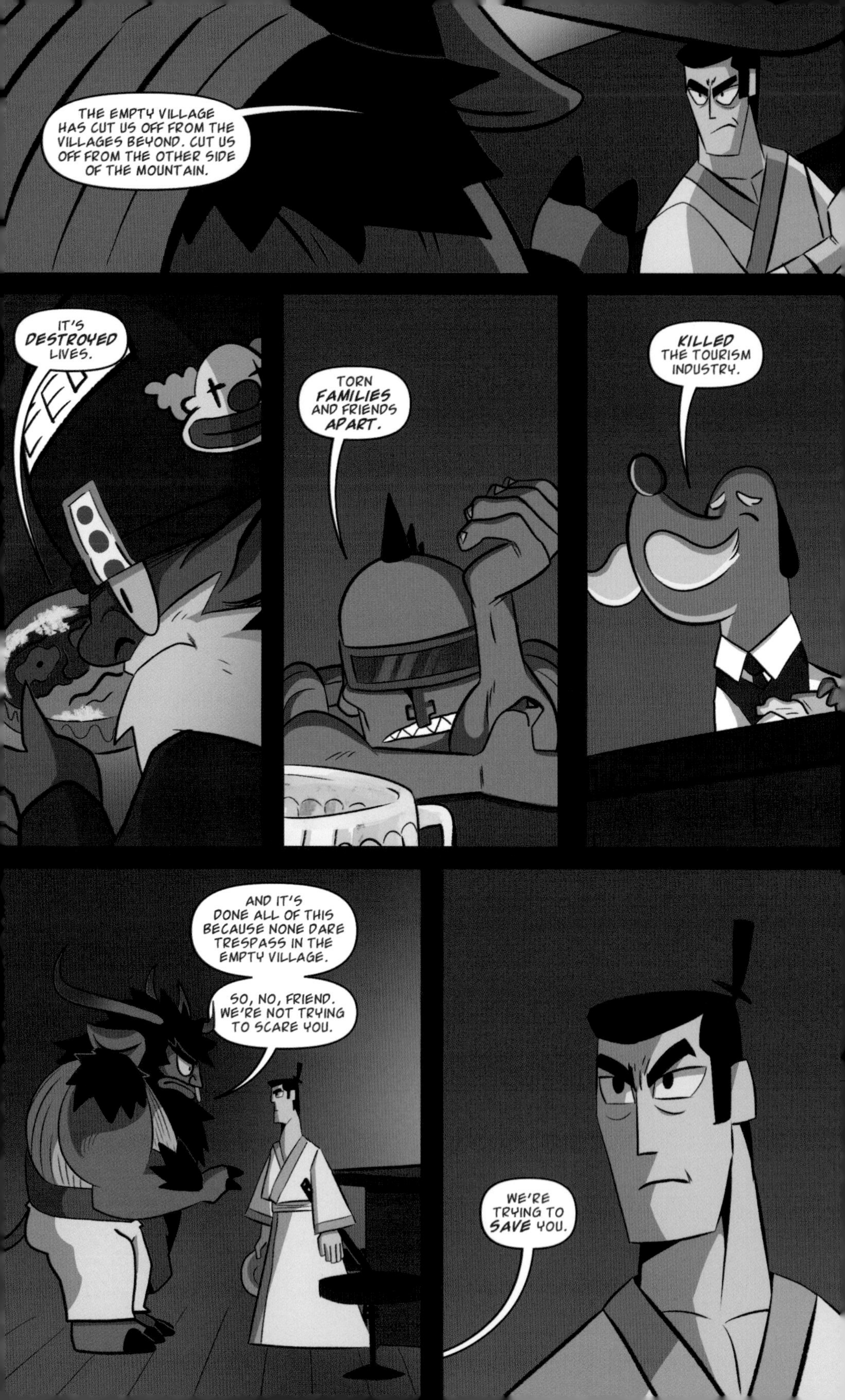

THE EMPTY VILLAGE HAS CUT US OFF FROM THE VILLAGES BEYOND. CUT US OFF FROM THE OTHER SIDE OF THE MOUNTAIN.
IT'S DESTROYED LIVES.
TORN FAMILIES AND FRIENDS APART.
KILLED THE TOURISM INDUSTRY.
AND IT'S DONE ALL OF THIS BECAUSE NONE DARE TRESPASS IN THE EMPTY VILLAGE.
SO, NO, FRIEND. WE'RE NOT TRYING TO SCARE YOU.
WE'RE TRYING TO SAVE YOU.

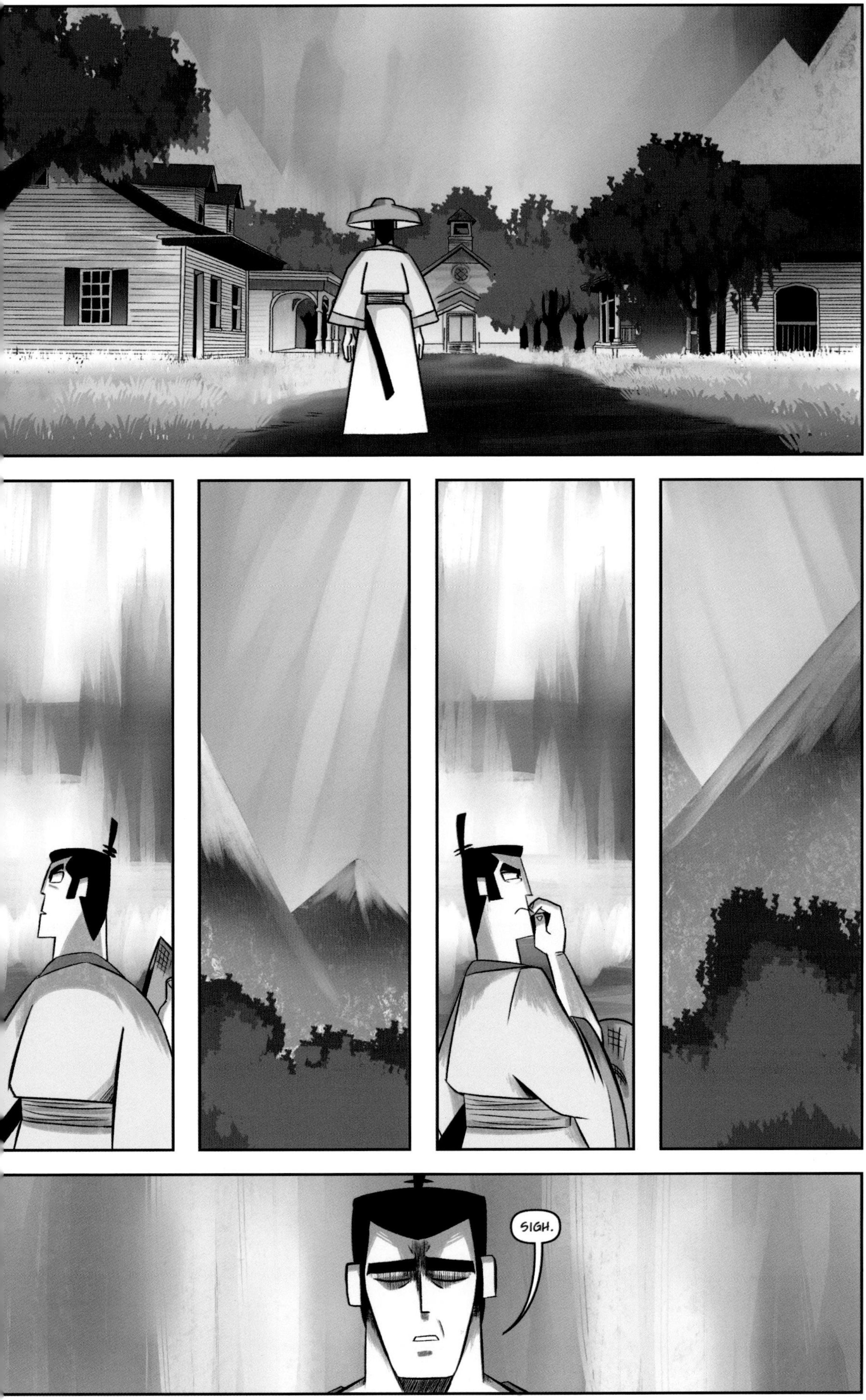
SIGH.

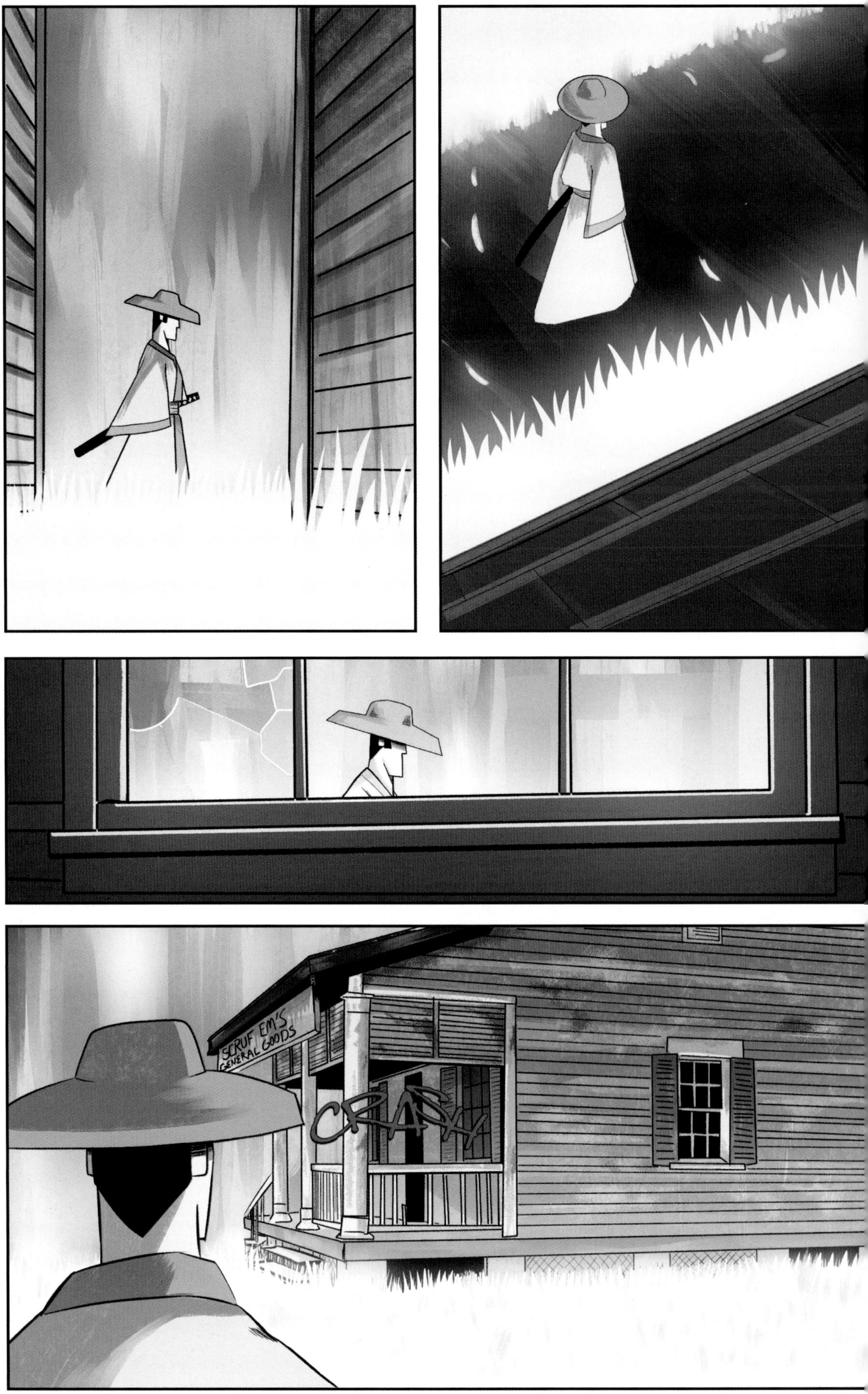
SCRUF EM'S
GENERAL GOODS
CRASH!

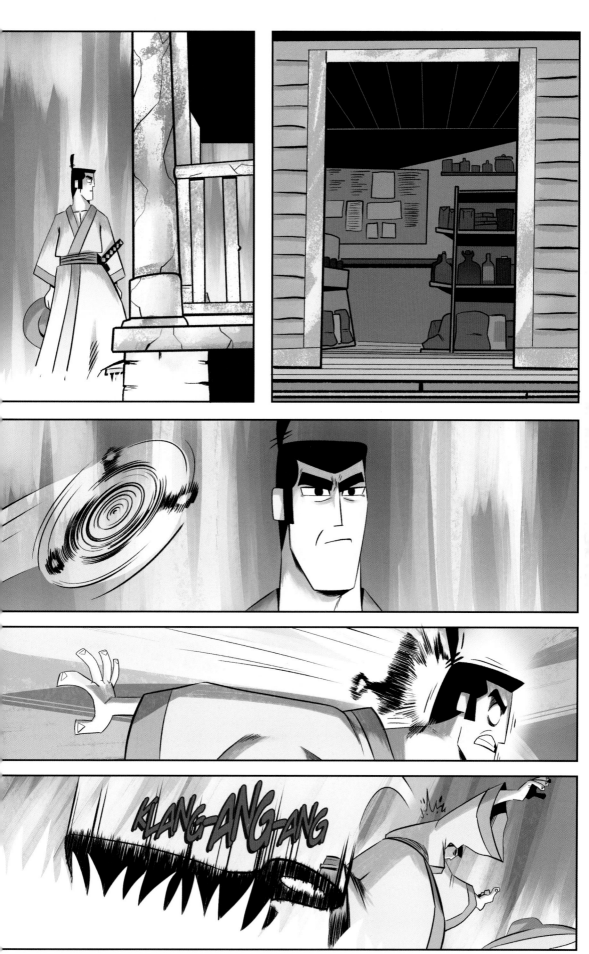

KLANG-ANG-ANG

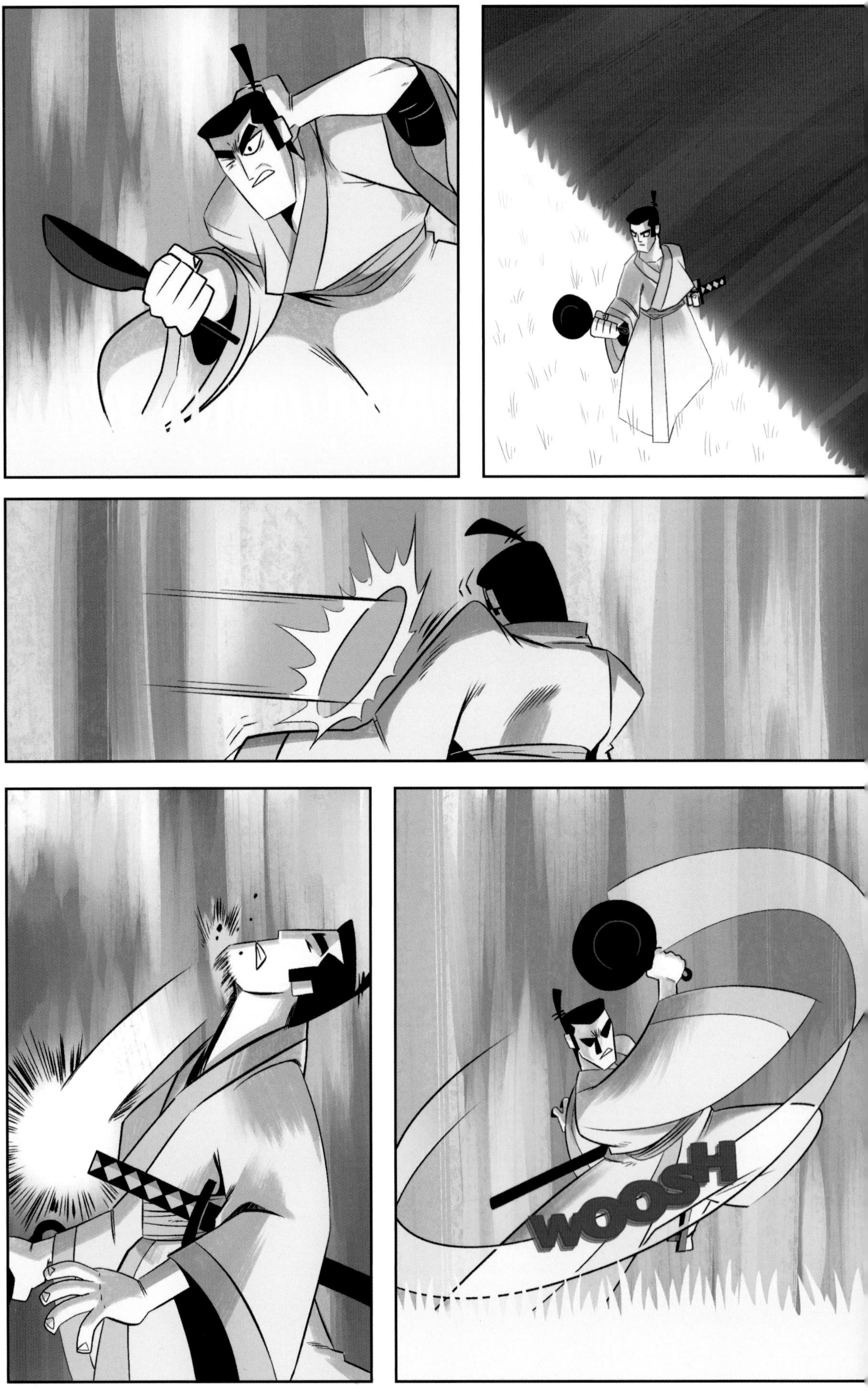
WOOSH

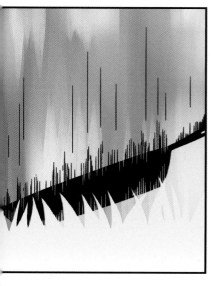

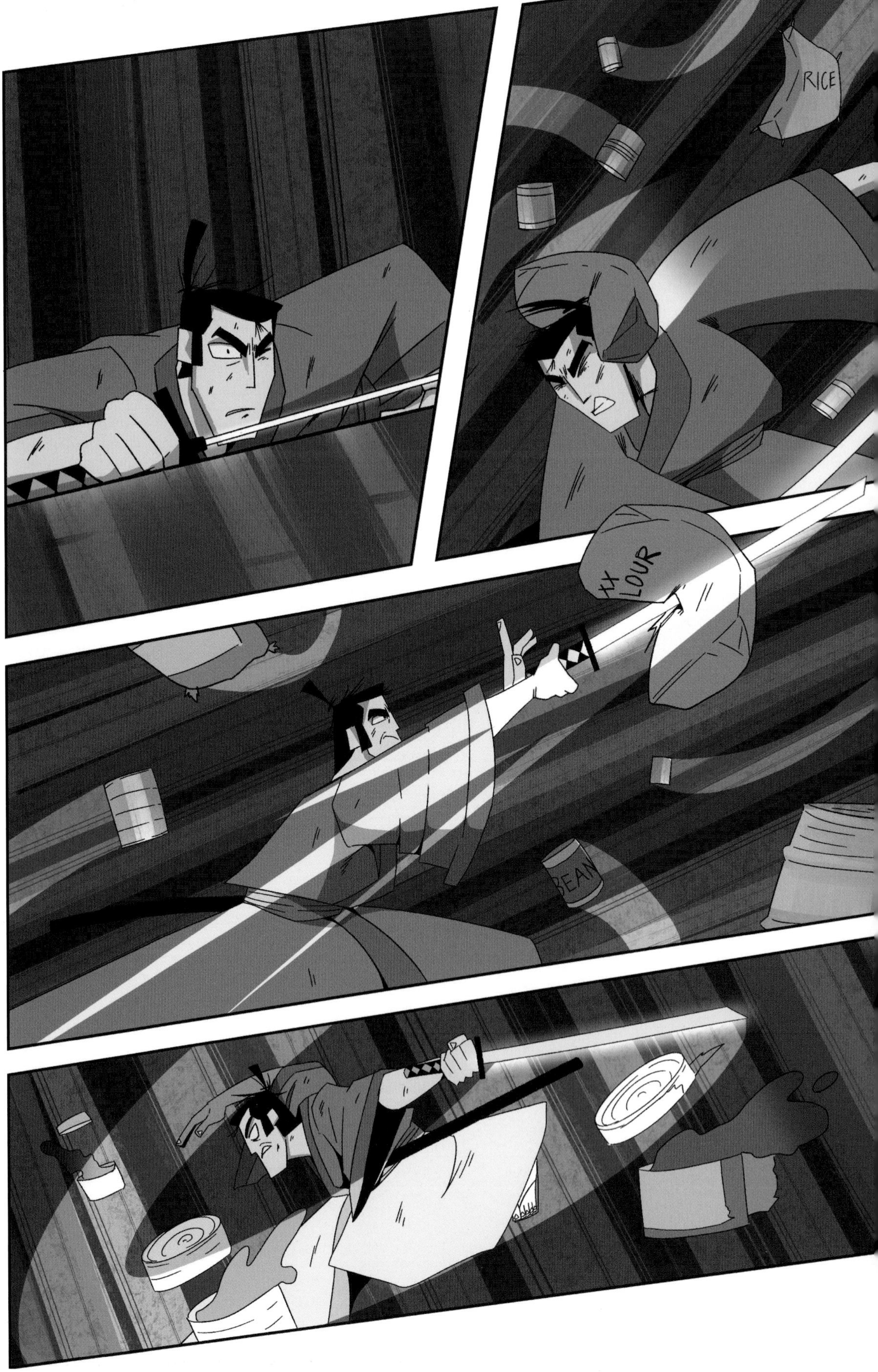

RICE
LOUR
BEAN

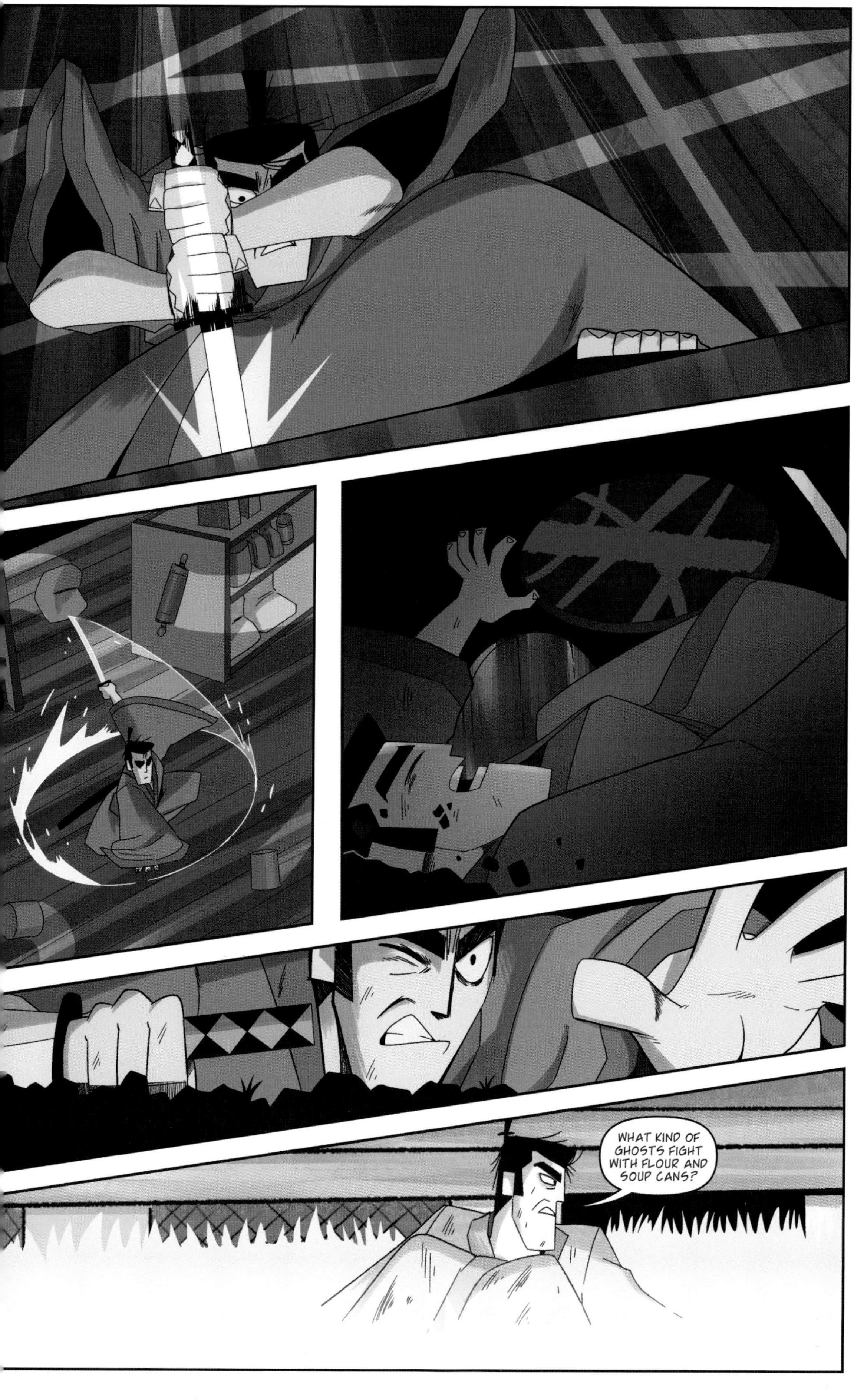
WHAT KIND OF GHOSTS FIGHT WITH FLOUR AND SOUP CANS?

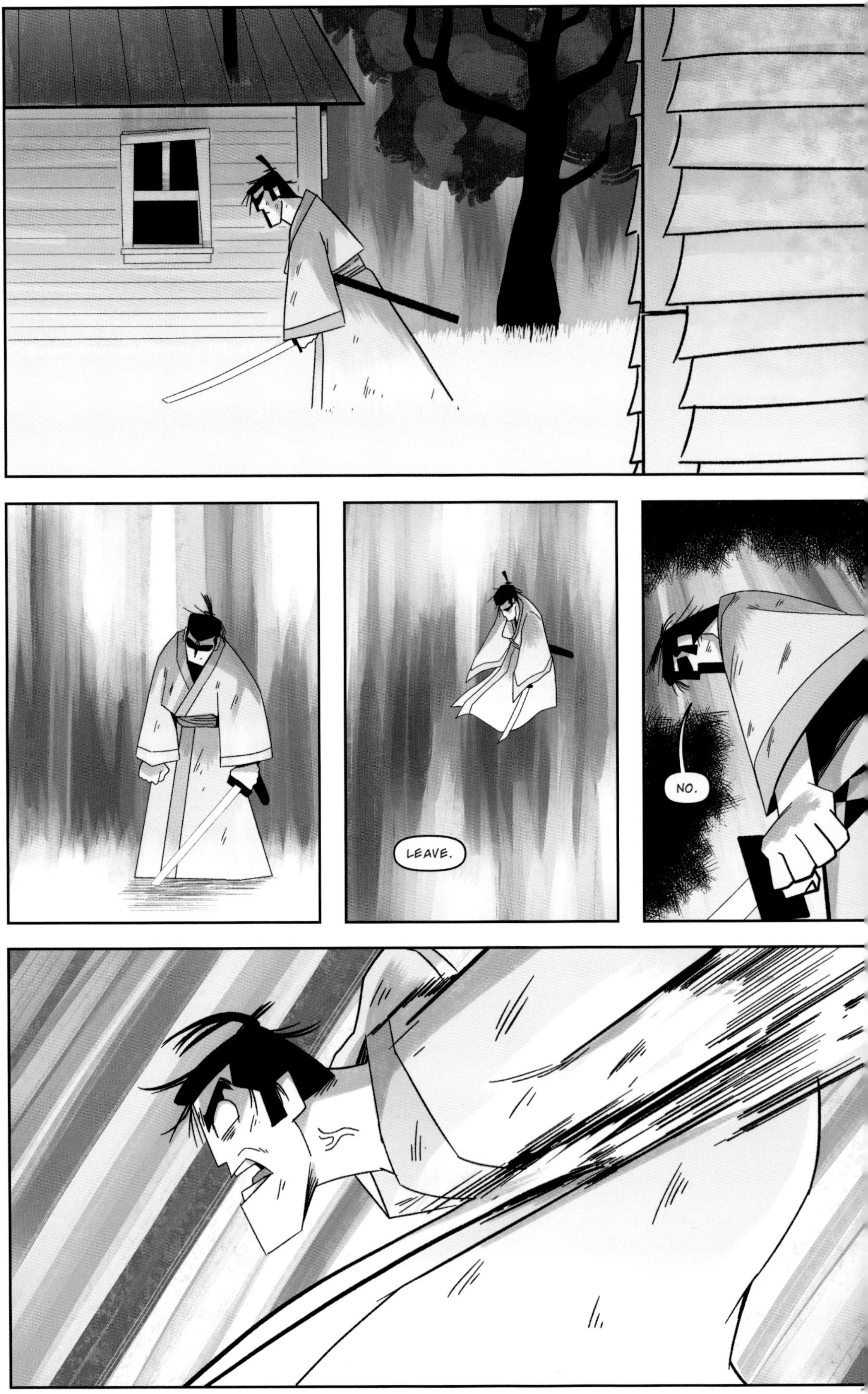
LEAVE.
NO.

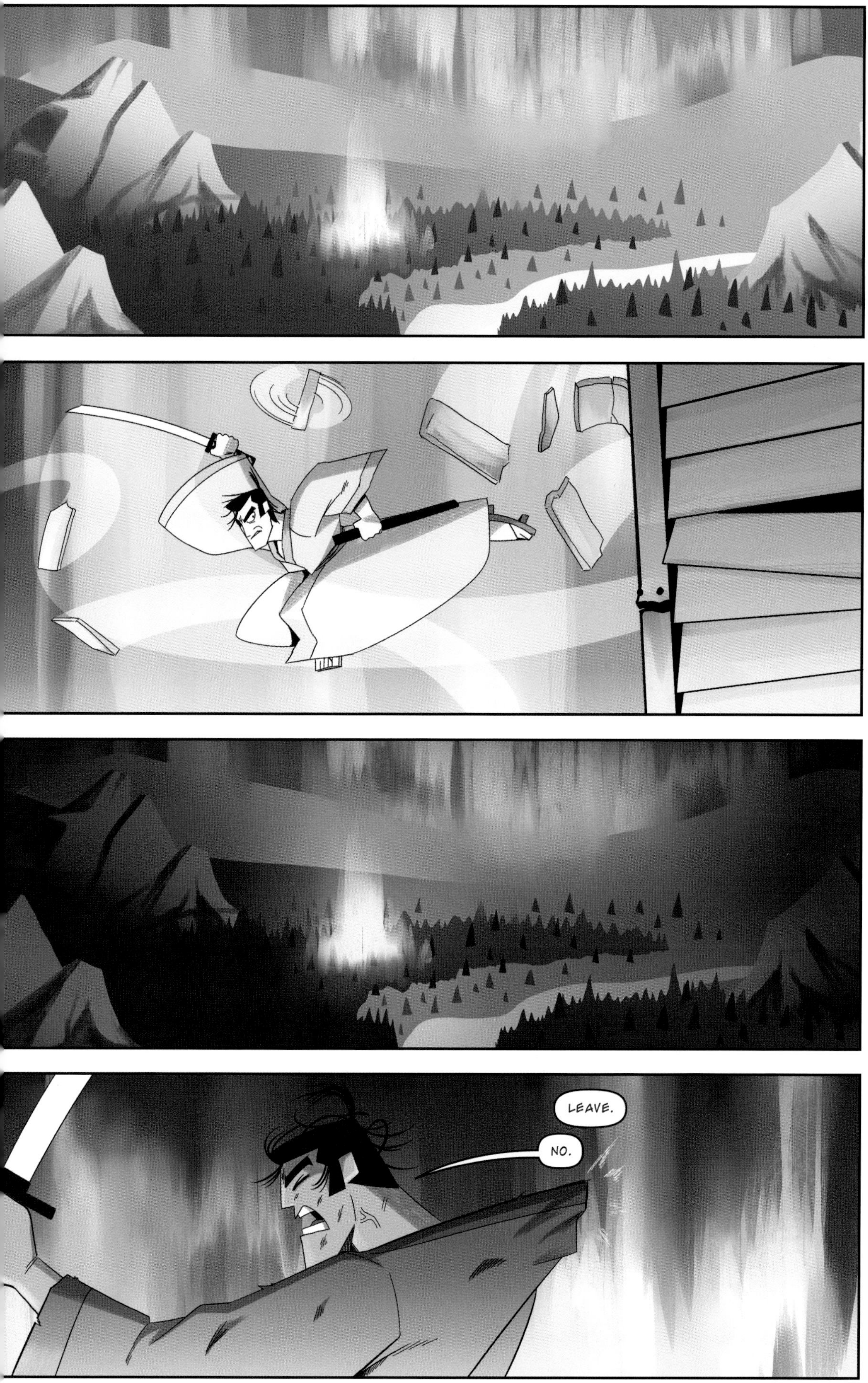
LEAVE.
NO.

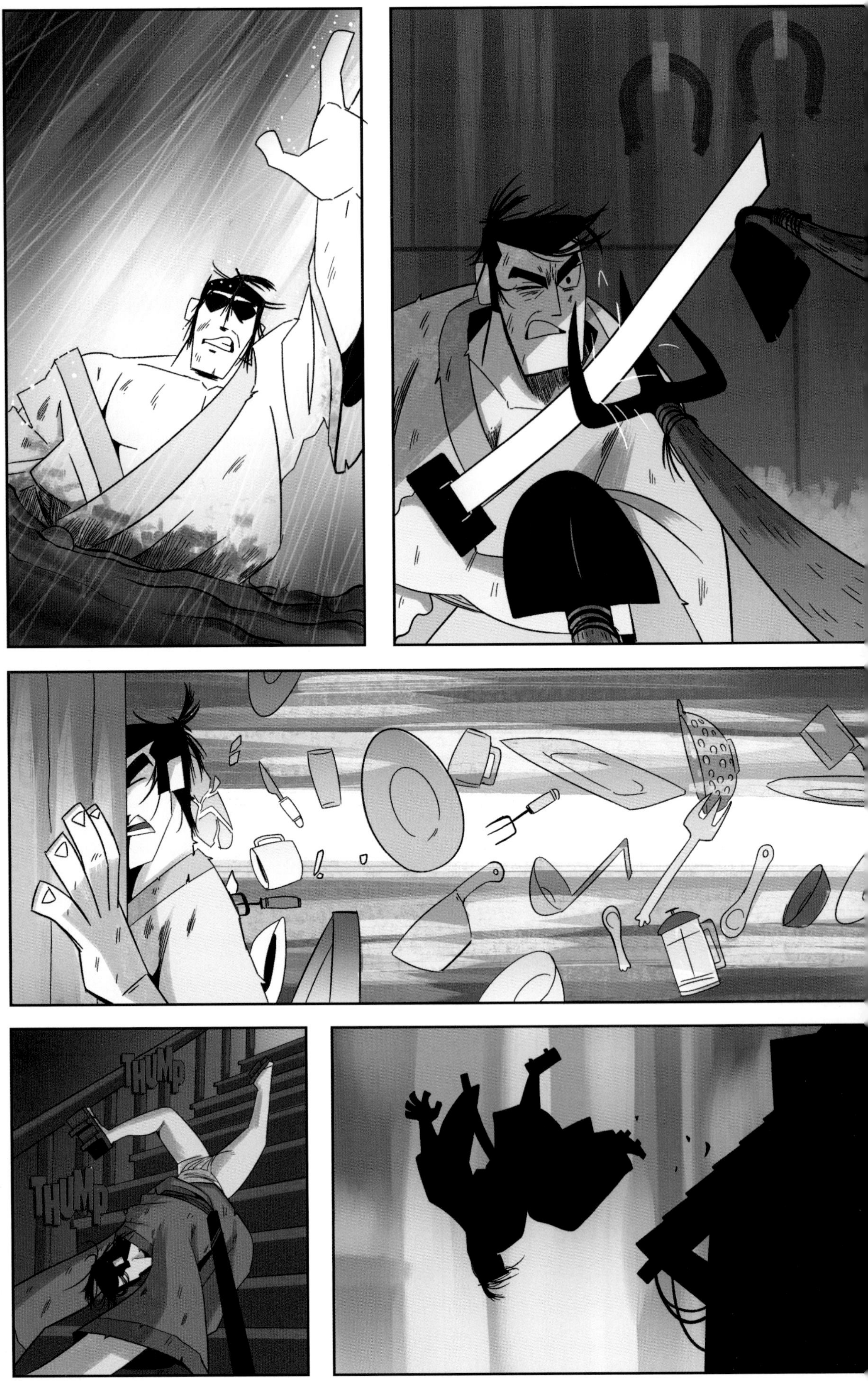
THUMP
THUMP

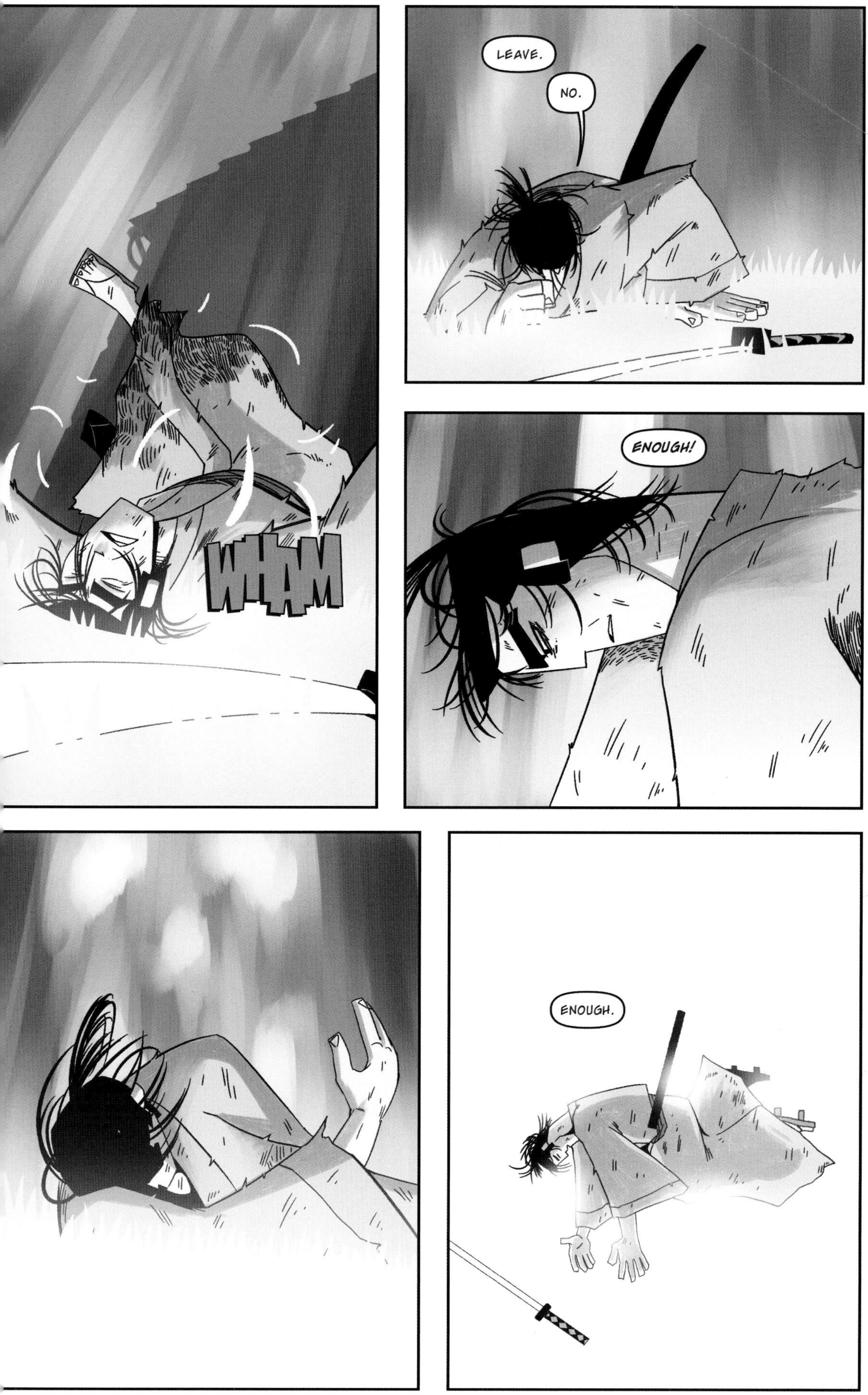
WHAM
LEAVE.
NO.
ENOUGH!
ENOUGH.

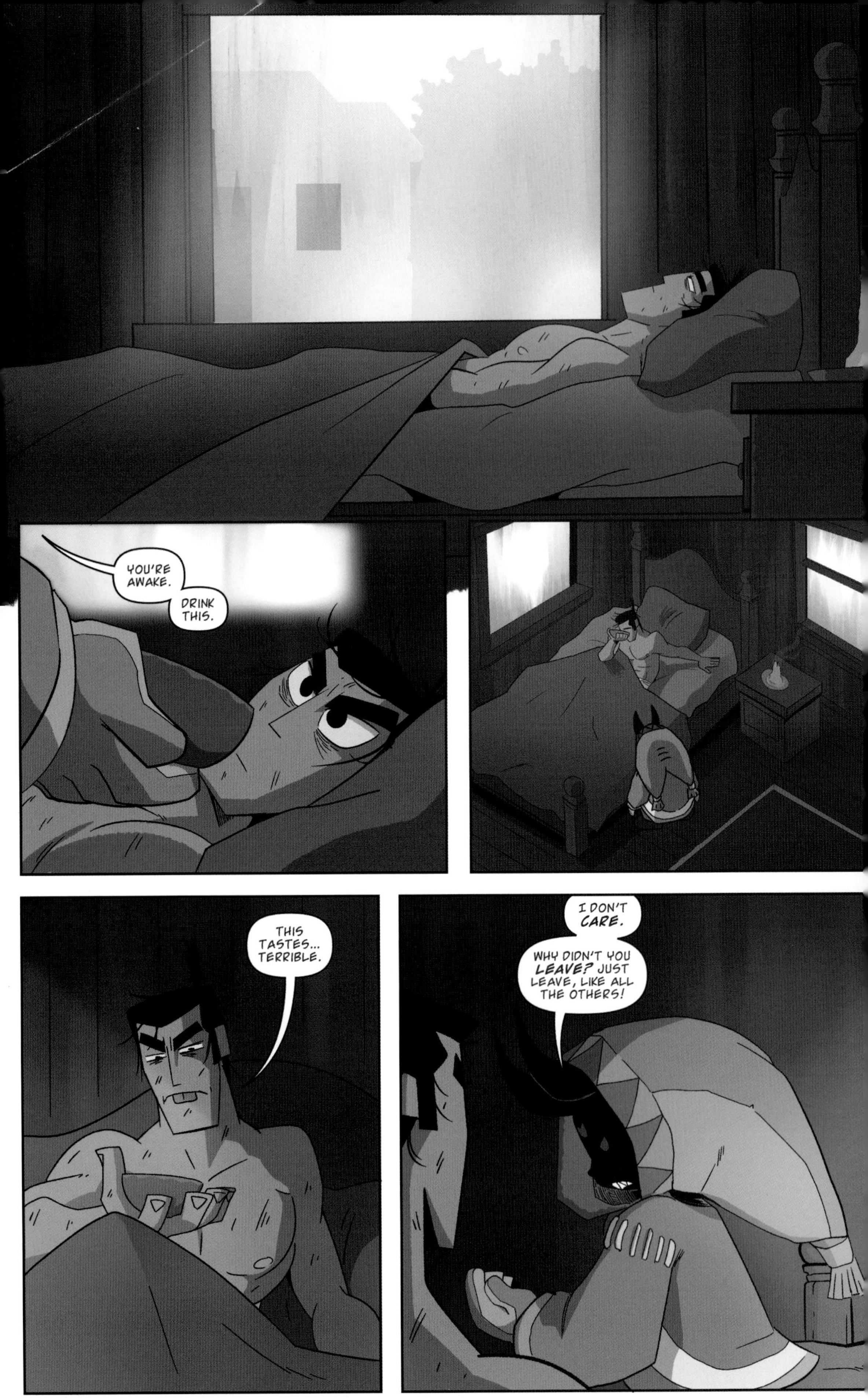
YOU'RE AWAKE.
DRINK THIS.
THIS TASTES... TERRIBLE.
I DON'T CARE.
WHY DIDN'T YOU LEAVE? JUST LEAVE, LIKE ALL THE OTHERS!

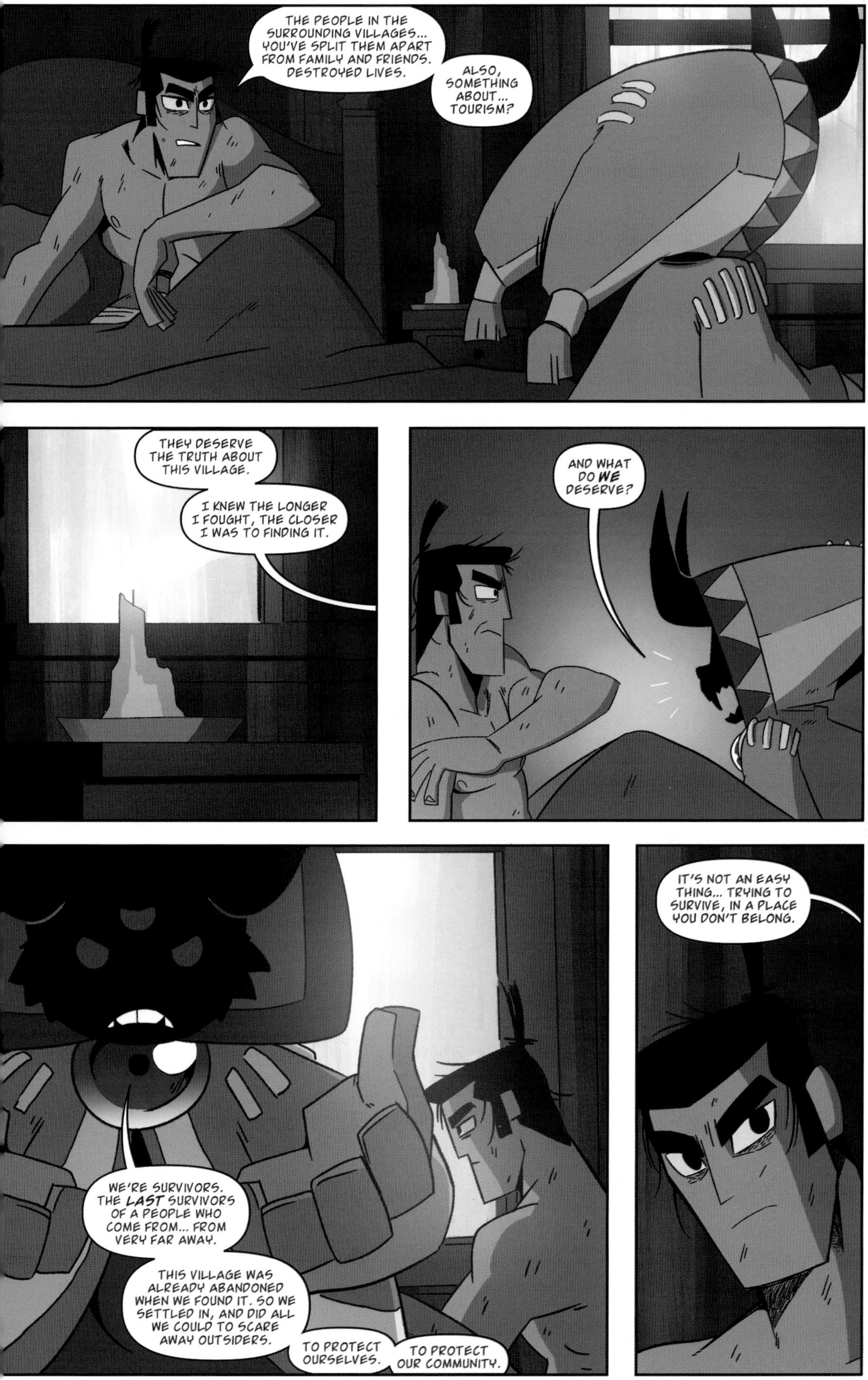
THE PEOPLE IN THE SURROUNDING VILLAGES... YOU'VE SPLIT THEM APART FROM FAMILY AND FRIENDS. DESTROYED LIVES.
ALSO, SOMETHING ABOUT... TOURISM?
THEY DESERVE THE TRUTH ABOUT THIS VILLAGE.
I KNEW THE LONGER I FOUGHT, THE CLOSER I WAS TO FINDING IT.
AND WHAT DO *WE* DESERVE?
WE'RE SURVIVORS. THE *LAST* SURVIVORS OF A PEOPLE WHO COME FROM... FROM VERY FAR AWAY.
THIS VILLAGE WAS ALREADY ABANDONED WHEN WE FOUND IT. SO WE SETTLED IN, AND DID ALL WE COULD TO SCARE AWAY OUTSIDERS.
TO PROTECT OURSELVES.
TO PROTECT OUR COMMUNITY.
IT'S NOT AN EASY THING... TRYING TO SURVIVE, IN A PLACE YOU DON'T BELONG.

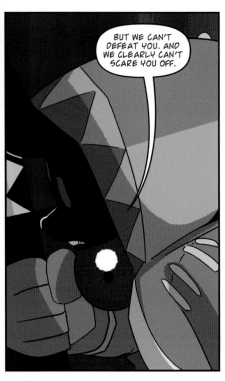

BUT WE CAN'T DEFEAT YOU. AND WE CLEARLY CAN'T SCARE YOU OFF.

SO WE ASK THAT YOU STOP FIGHTING. AND LEAVE OUR VILLAGE, PEACEFULLY.

"AFTER THAT...

"...OUR FATE IS IN YOUR HANDS."

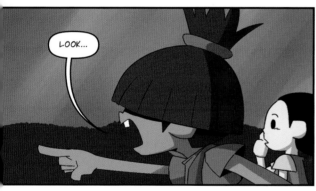

LOOK...

THAT MAN...
IS HE COMING
FROM...

HE IS.

CHILDREN!

CHILDREN,
STOP!

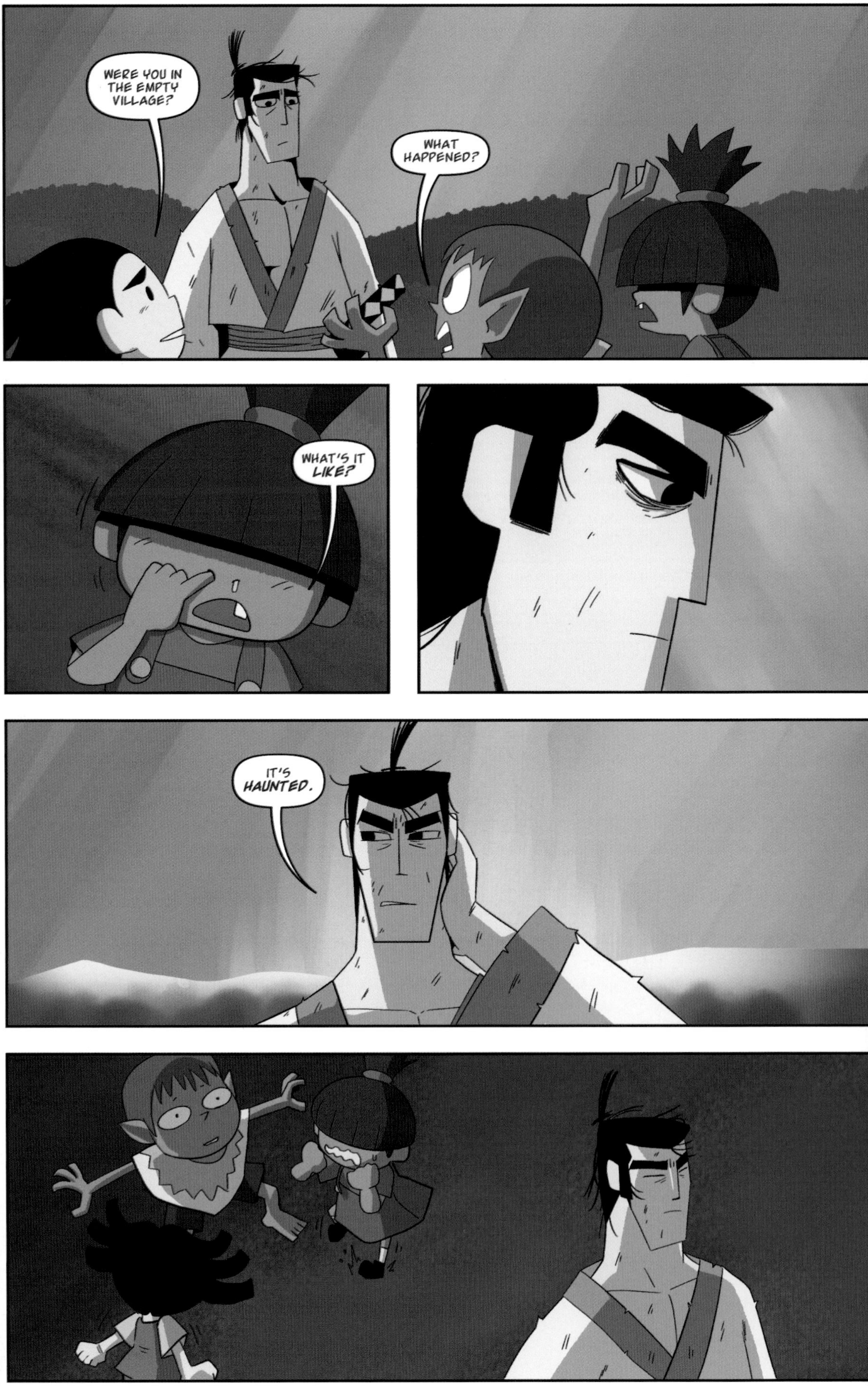
WERE YOU IN THE EMPTY VILLAGE?
WHAT HAPPENED?
WHAT'S IT LIKE?
IT'S HAUNTED.

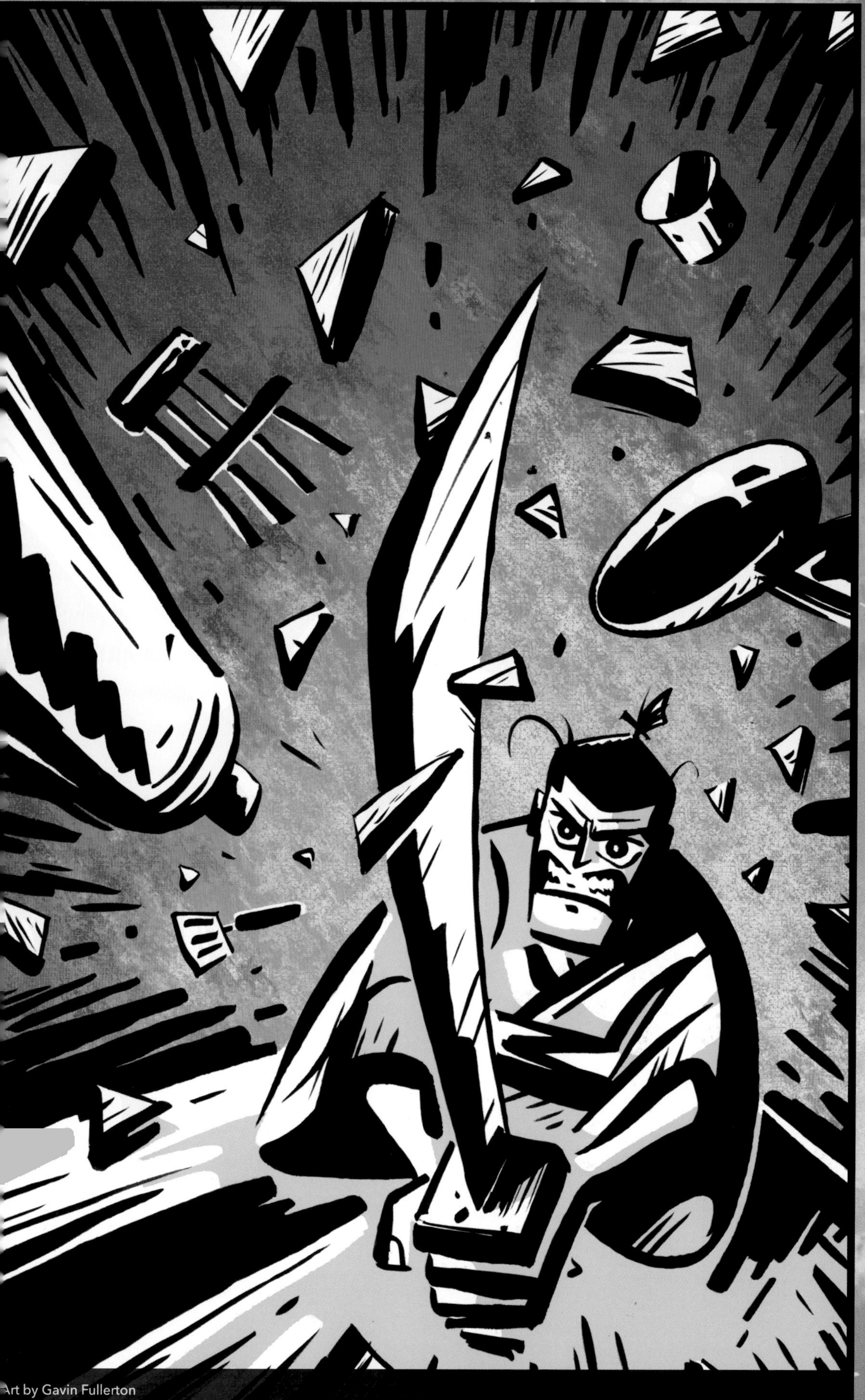

Art by Gavin Fullerton

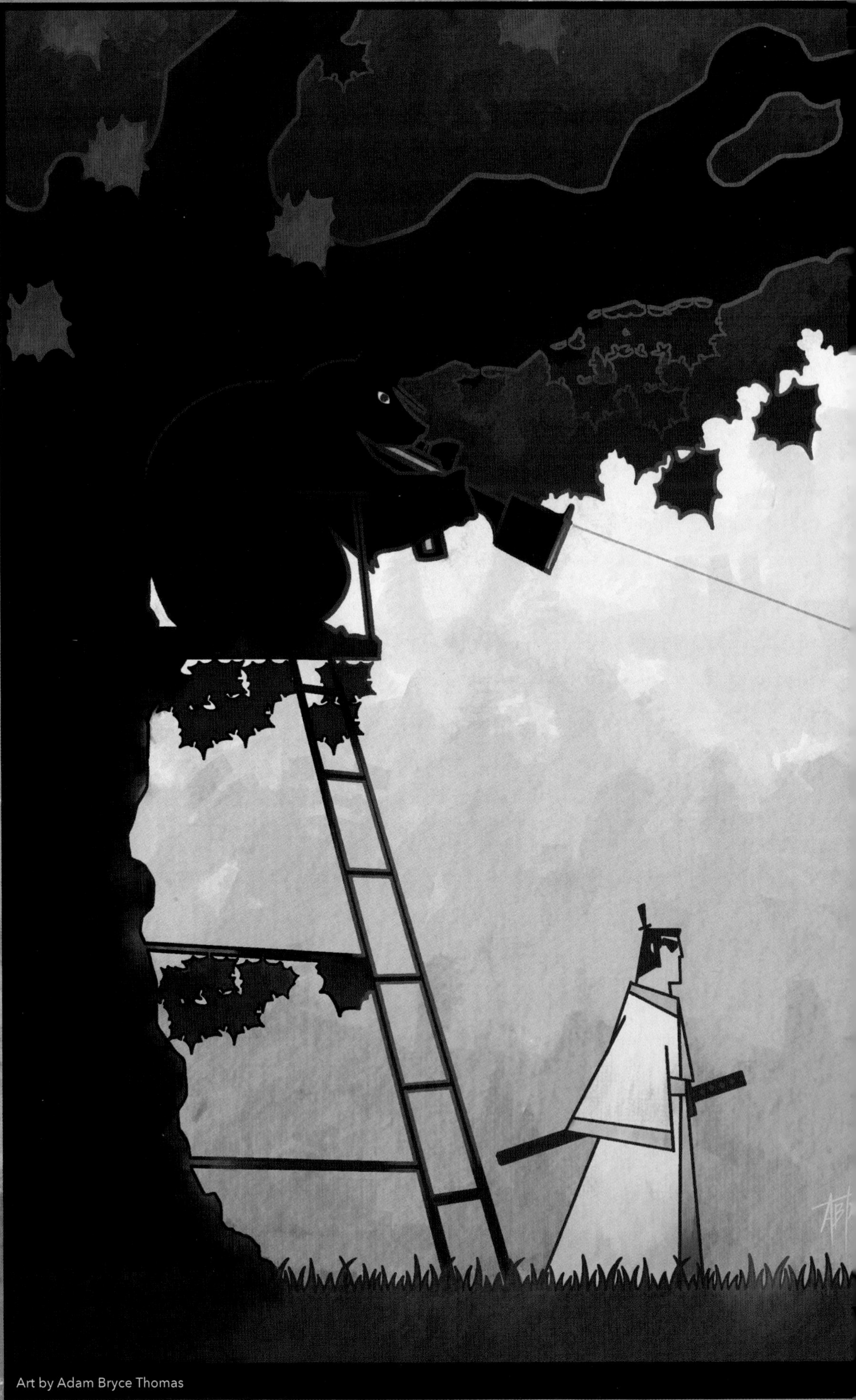

Art by Adam Bryce Thomas

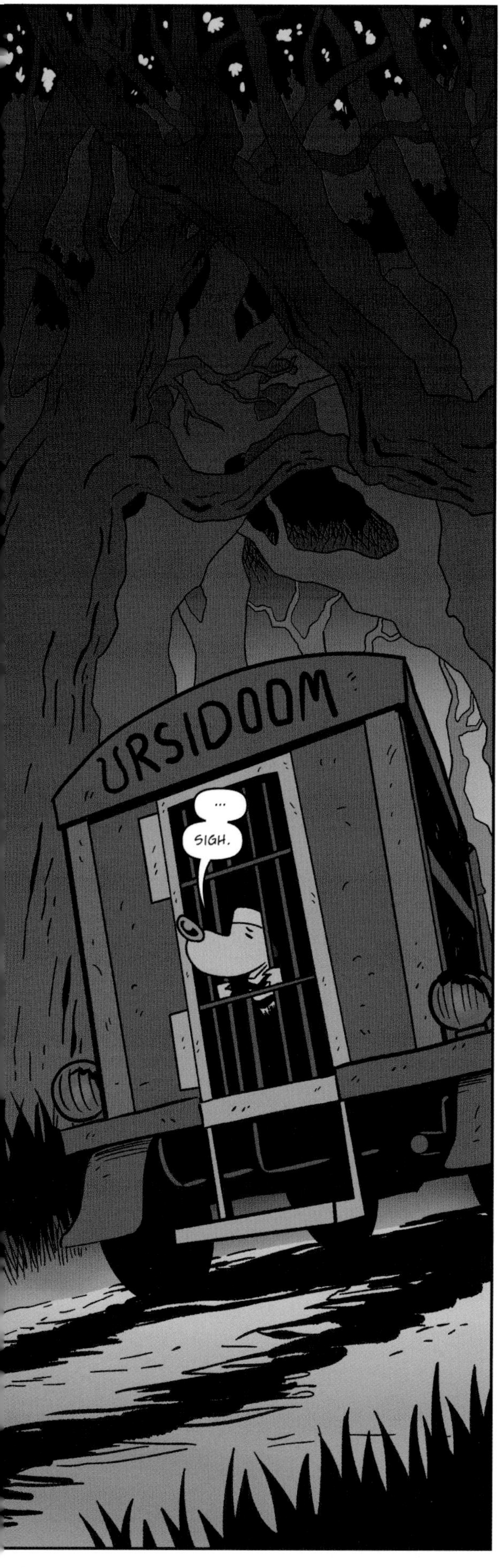
URSIDOOM
...
SIGH.

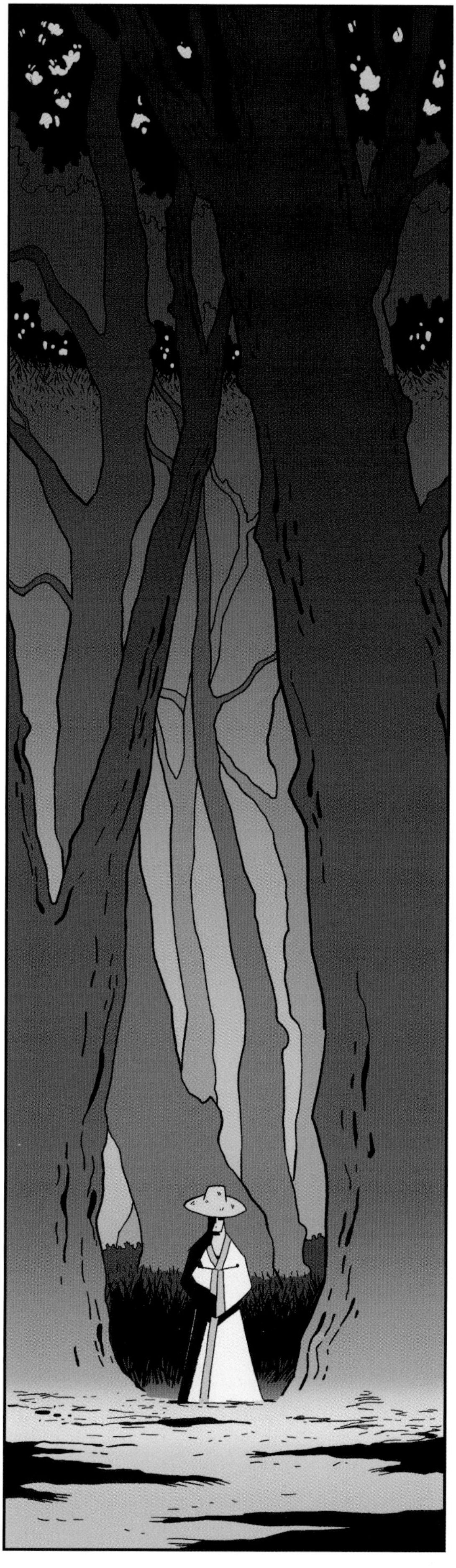

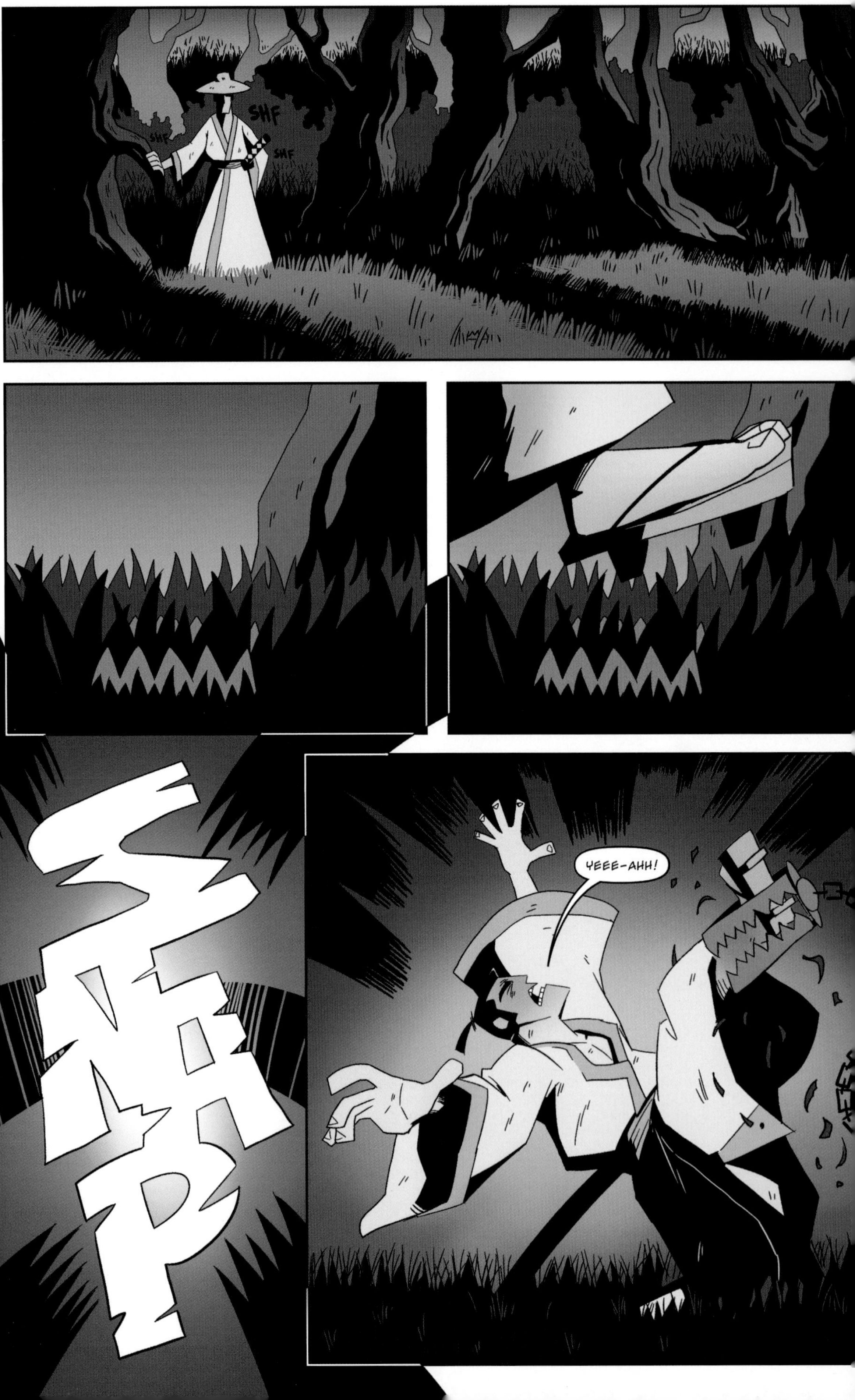
SHF
SHF
SHF
SNAP
YEEE-AHH!

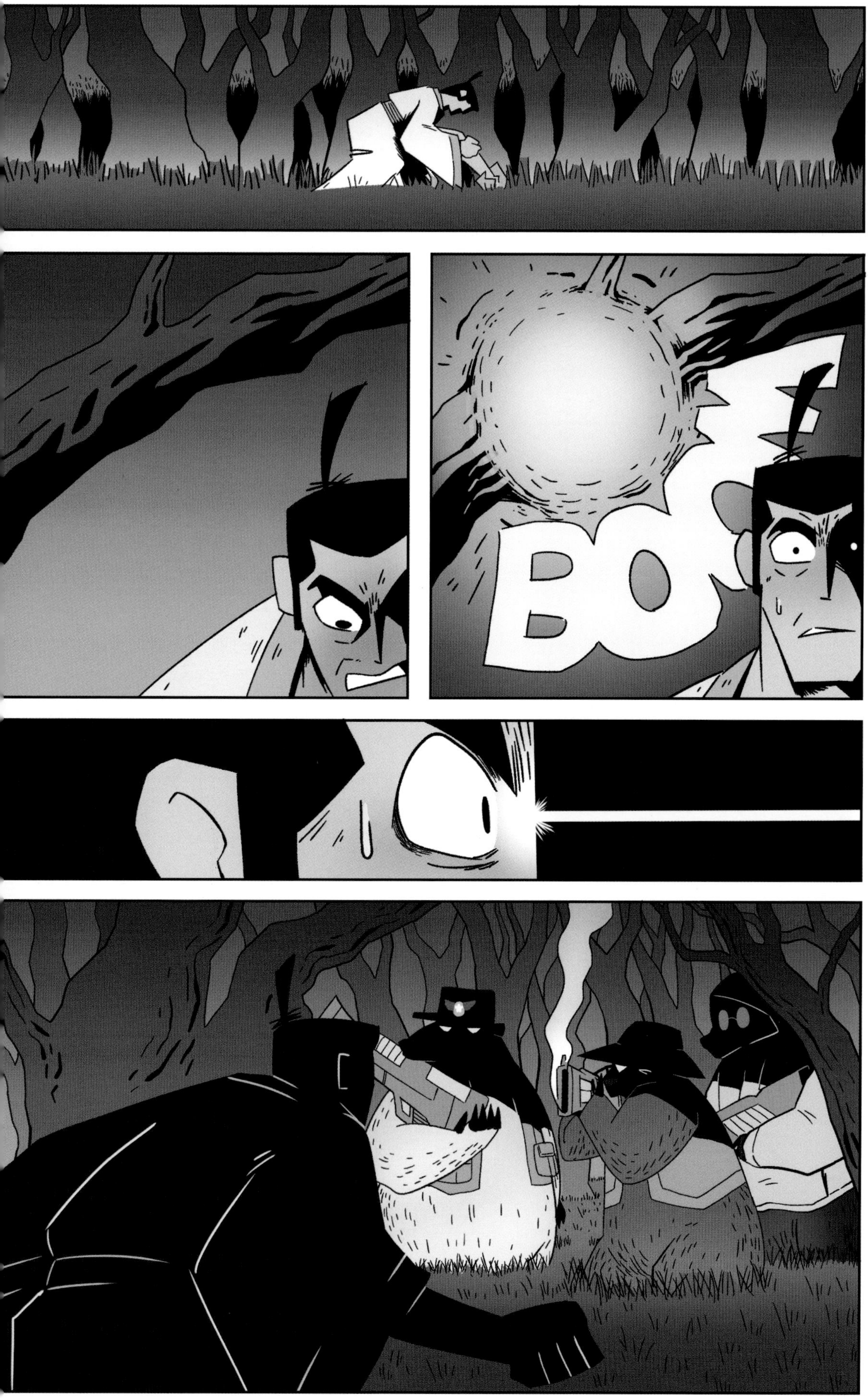
BO

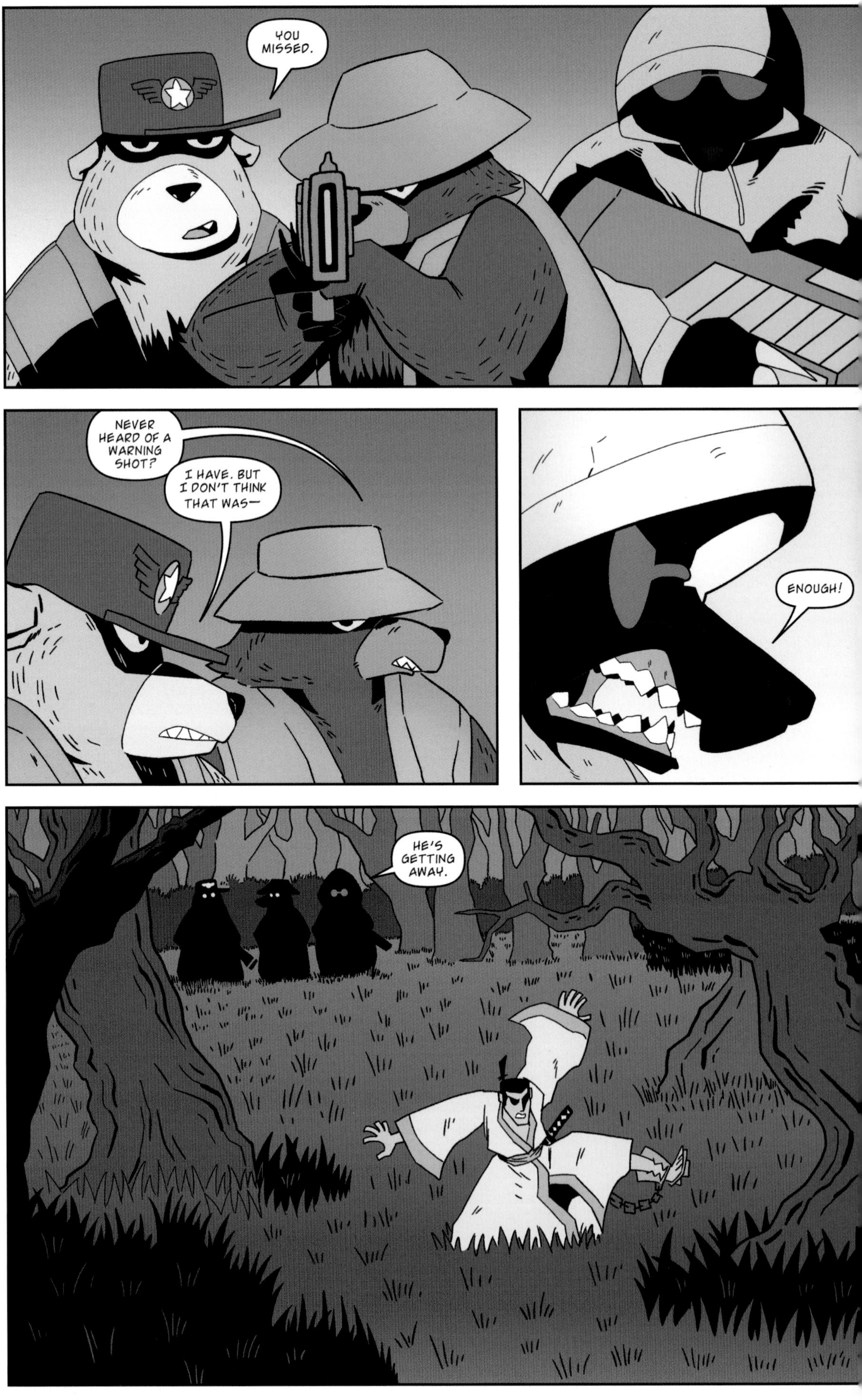
YOU MISSED.
NEVER HEARD OF A WARNING SHOT?
I HAVE. BUT I DON'T THINK THAT WAS—
ENOUGH!
HE'S GETTING AWAY.

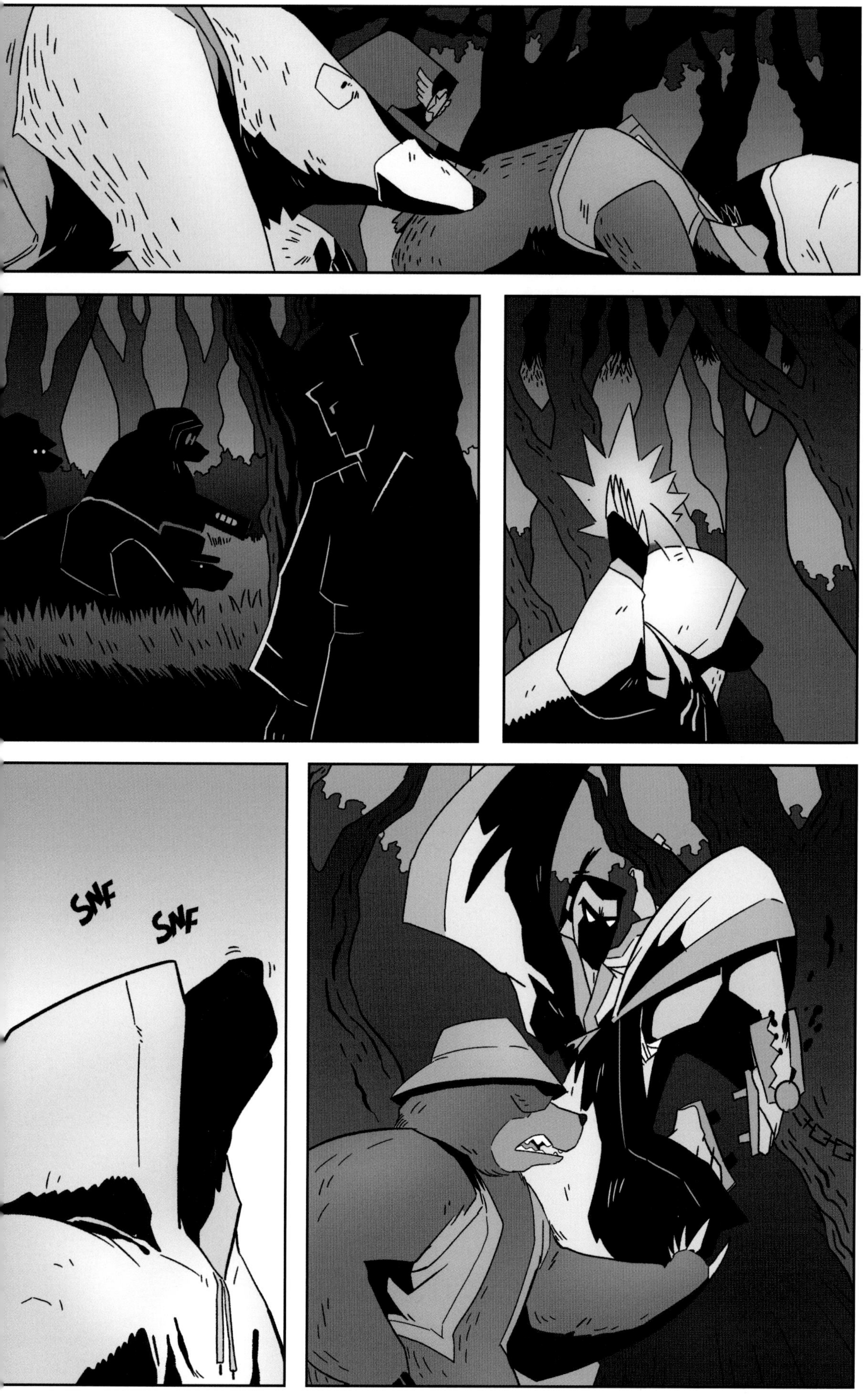
SNF
SNF

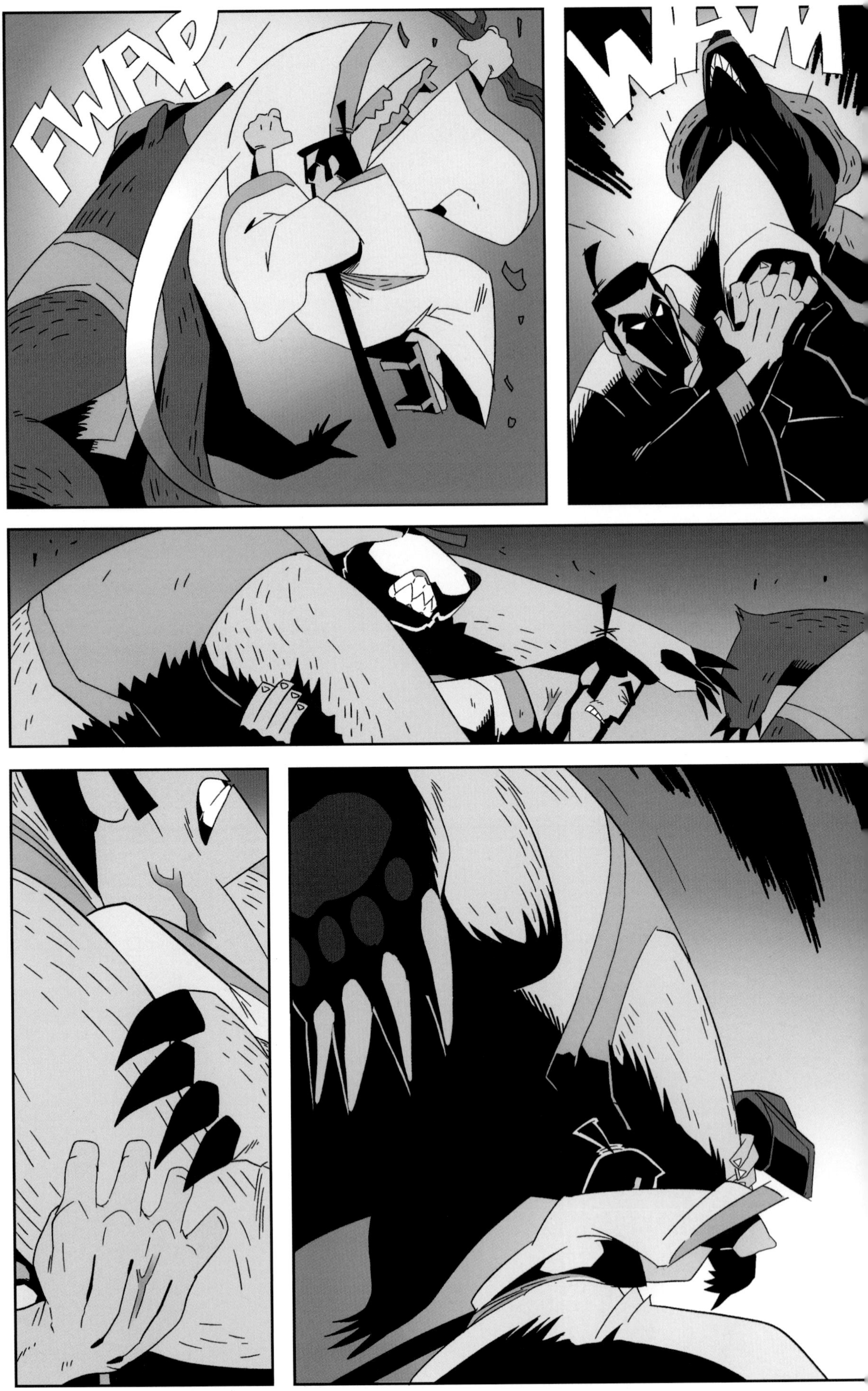
FWAP
WHAM

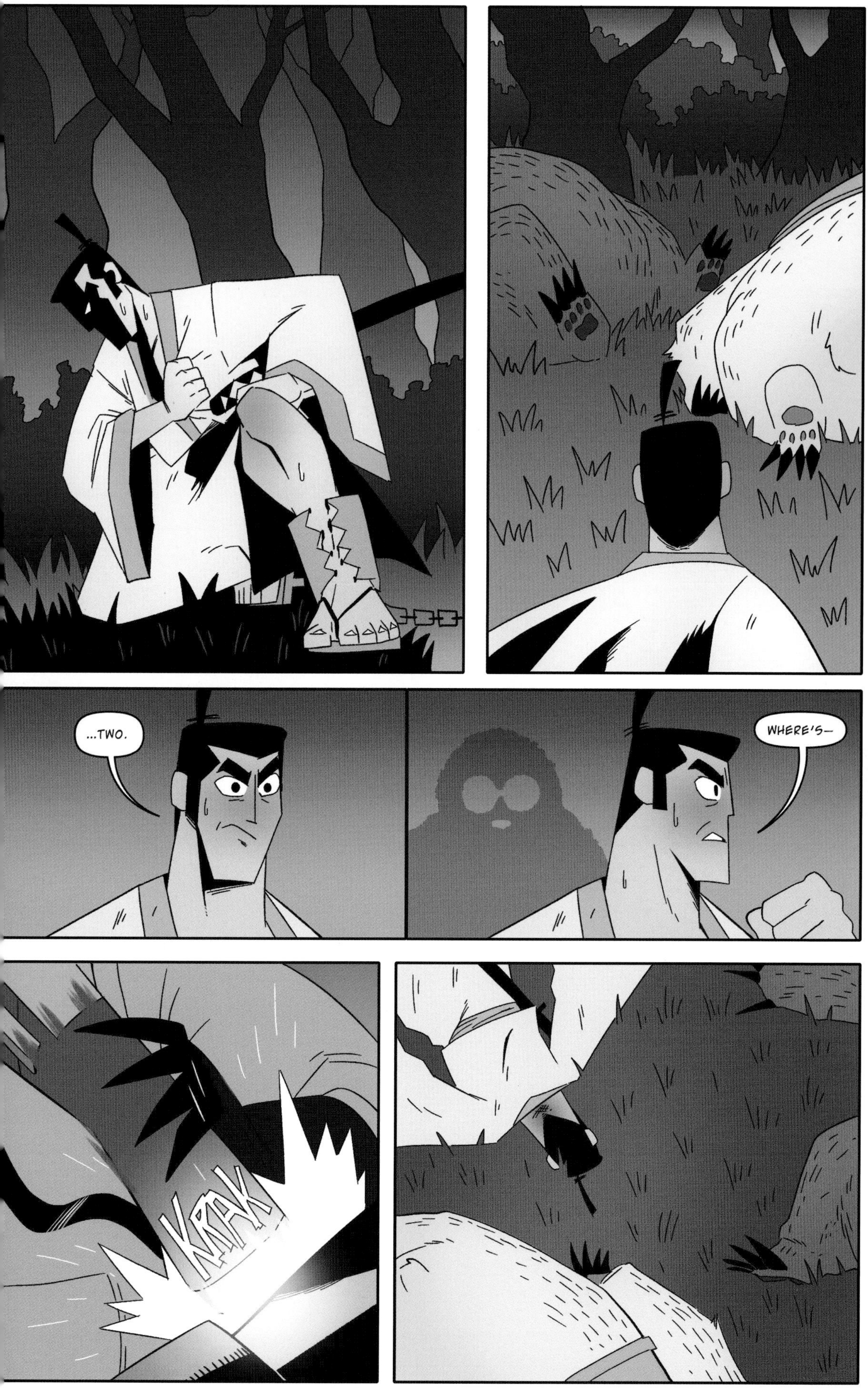
...TWO.
WHERE'S—
KRAK

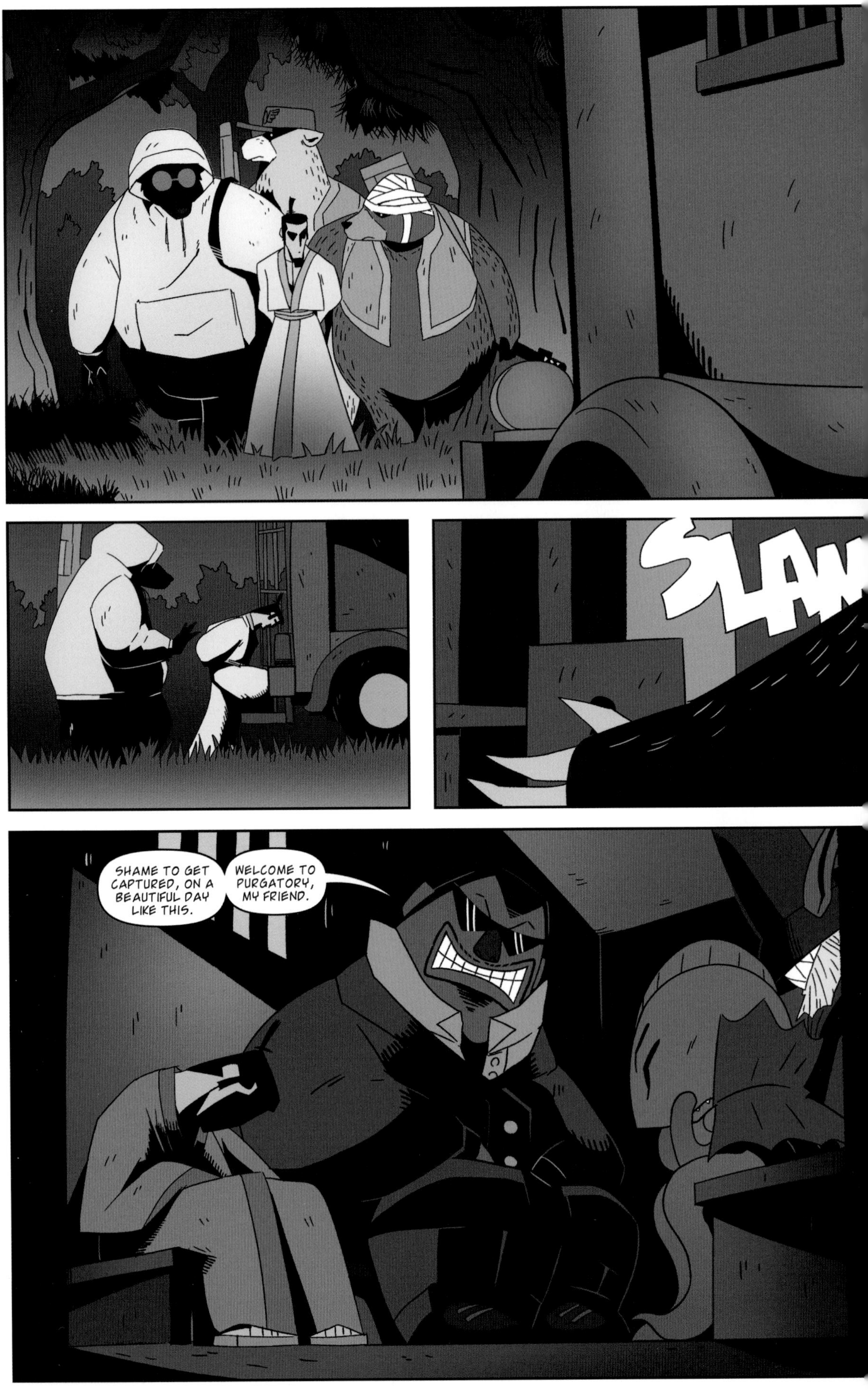
WELCOME TO PURGATORY, MY FRIEND.
SHAME TO GET CAPTURED, ON A BEAUTIFUL DAY LIKE THIS.

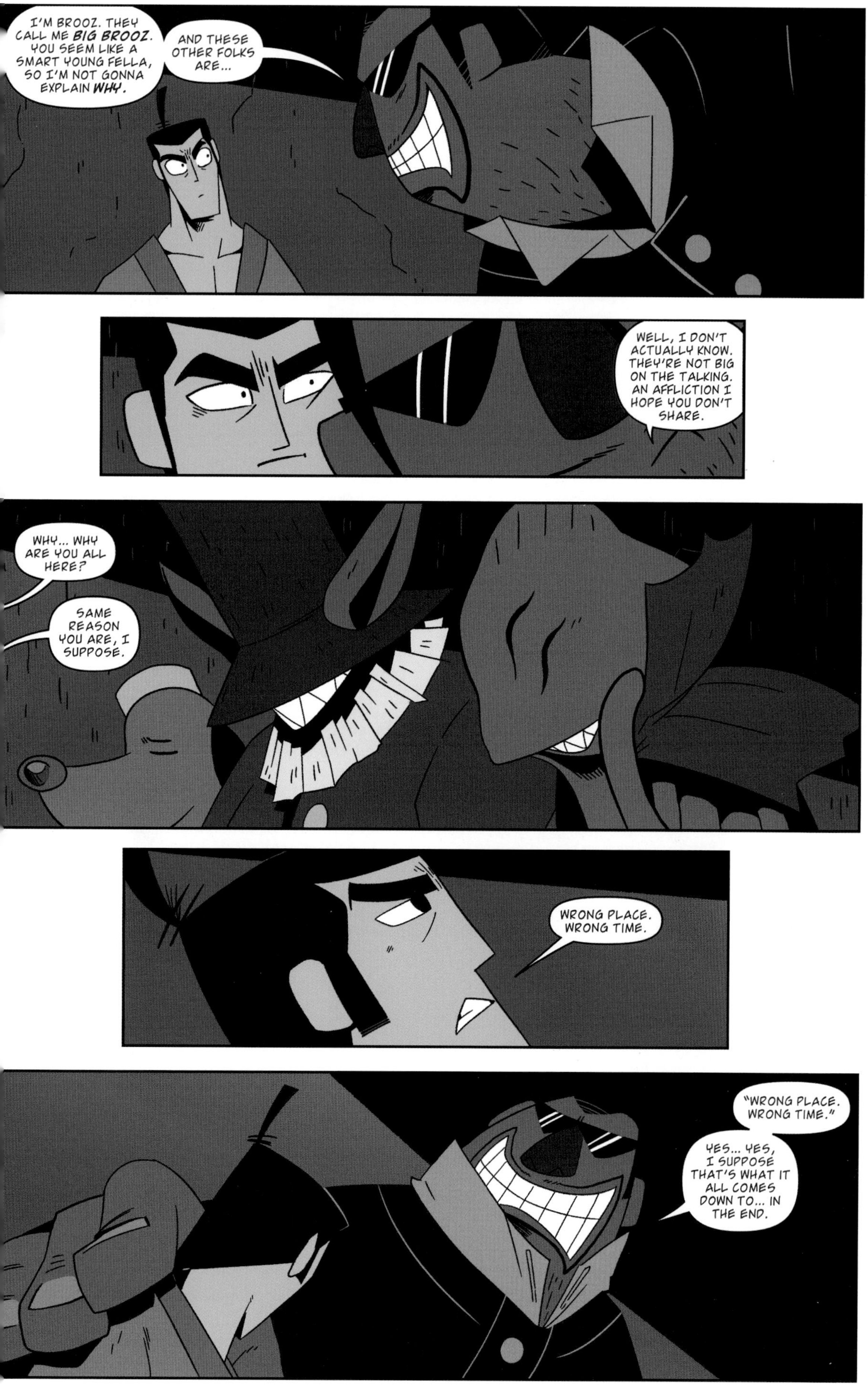

I'M BROOZ. THEY CALL ME **BIG BROOZ**. YOU SEEM LIKE A SMART YOUNG FELLA, SO I'M NOT GONNA EXPLAIN **WHY**.
AND THESE OTHER FOLKS ARE...
WELL, I DON'T ACTUALLY KNOW. THEY'RE NOT BIG ON THE TALKING. AN AFFLICTION I HOPE YOU DON'T SHARE.
WHY... WHY ARE YOU ALL HERE?
SAME REASON YOU ARE, I SUPPOSE.
WRONG PLACE. WRONG TIME.
"WRONG PLACE. WRONG TIME."
YES... YES, I SUPPOSE THAT'S WHAT IT ALL COMES DOWN TO... IN THE END.

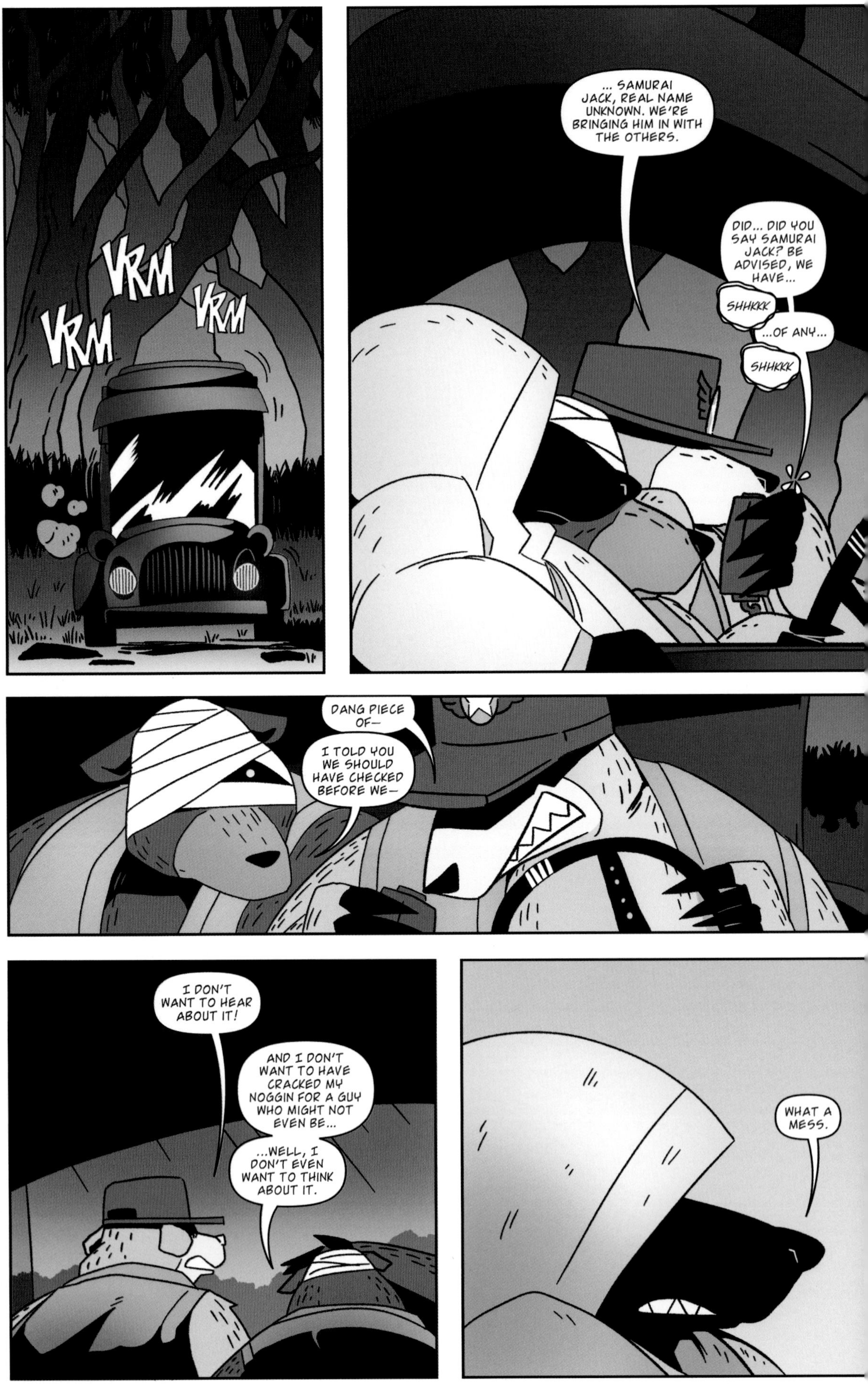
VRM
VRM
VRM
... SAMURAI JACK, REAL NAME UNKNOWN. WE'RE BRINGING HIM IN WITH THE OTHERS.
DID... DID YOU SAY SAMURAI JACK? BE ADVISED, WE HAVE...
SHHKKK
...OF ANY...
SHHKKK
DANG PIECE OF—
I TOLD YOU WE SHOULD HAVE CHECKED BEFORE WE—
I DON'T WANT TO HEAR ABOUT IT!
AND I DON'T WANT TO HAVE CRACKED MY NOGGIN FOR A GUY WHO MIGHT NOT EVEN BE...
...WELL, I DON'T EVEN WANT TO THINK ABOUT IT.
WHAT A MESS.

—WHICH IS WHY THAT'S NOT SOMETHING I SHARE WITH MOST PEOPLE.

BUT THE MOMENT I SAW YOU, YOU STRUCK ME AS A FELLOW VOYAGER INTO THE SORTS OF IN-BETWEEN SPACES THAT WOULD MAKE MOST MEN—

—WELL, AND MOST WOMEN. I DON'T MEAN TO BE THE NON-INCLUSIVE TYPE. BUT ANYWAY—

DOES YOUR SHIRT HAVE A COLLAR STAY?

WHAT'S THAT? UH, YES, ACTUALLY. YES, IT DOES.

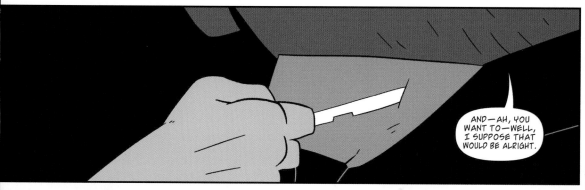

AND—AH, YOU WANT TO—WELL, I SUPPOSE THAT WOULD BE ALRIGHT.

SO, HOW LONG HAVE YOU BEEN IN THIS PARTICULAR IN-BETWEEN SPACE?

I'M FAIRLY NEW TO IT MYSELF, WHICH IS I SUPPOSE WHY I ALLOWED MYSELF TO FIND MYSELF IN THIS UNFORTUNATE—

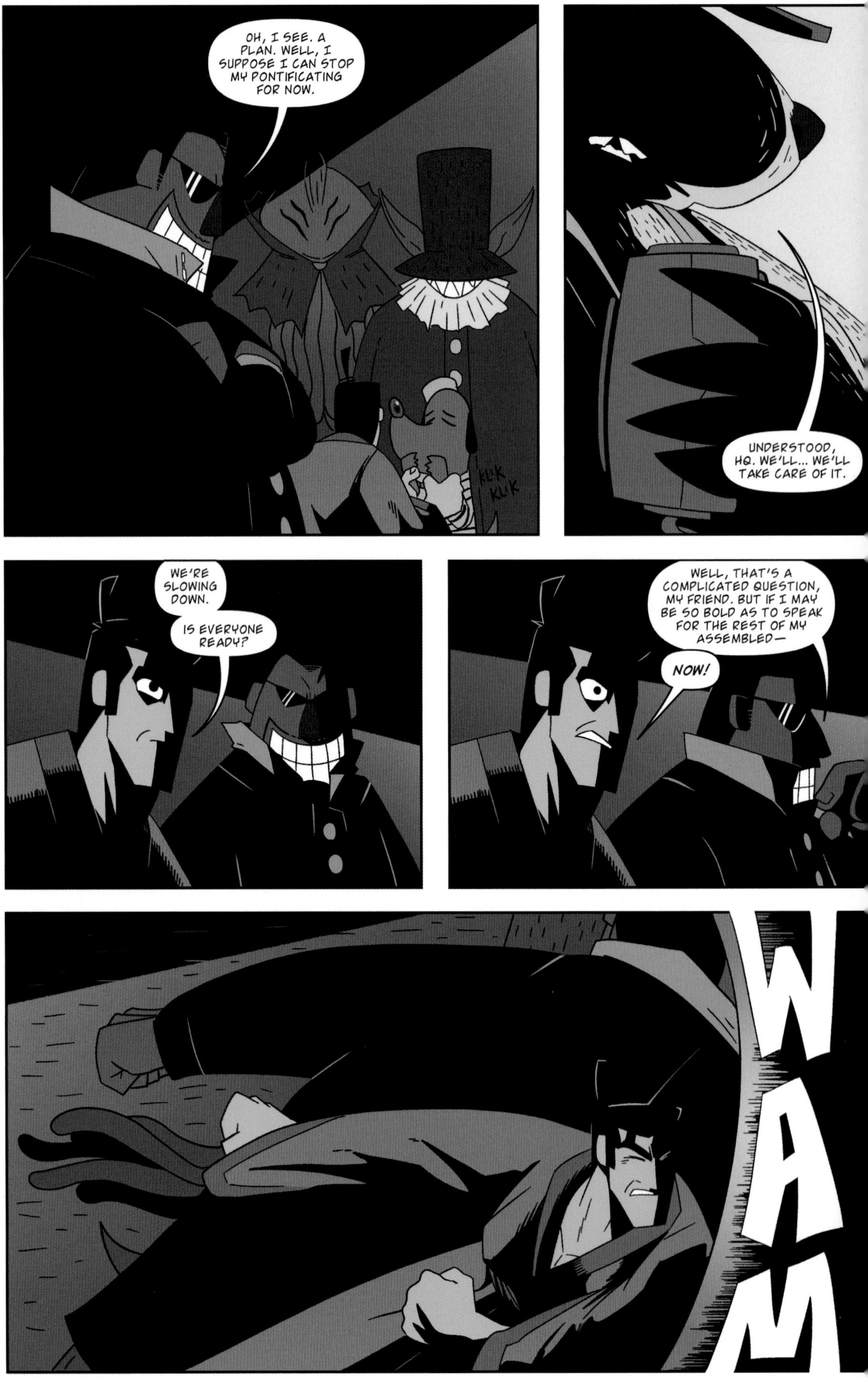
OH, I SEE. A PLAN. WELL, I SUPPOSE I CAN STOP MY PONTIFICATING FOR NOW.
KLIK KLIK
UNDERSTOOD, HQ. WE'LL... WE'LL TAKE CARE OF IT.
WE'RE SLOWING DOWN.
IS EVERYONE READY?
WELL, THAT'S A COMPLICATED QUESTION, MY FRIEND. BUT IF I MAY BE SO BOLD AS TO SPEAK FOR THE REST OF MY ASSEMBLED—
NOW!
WAM

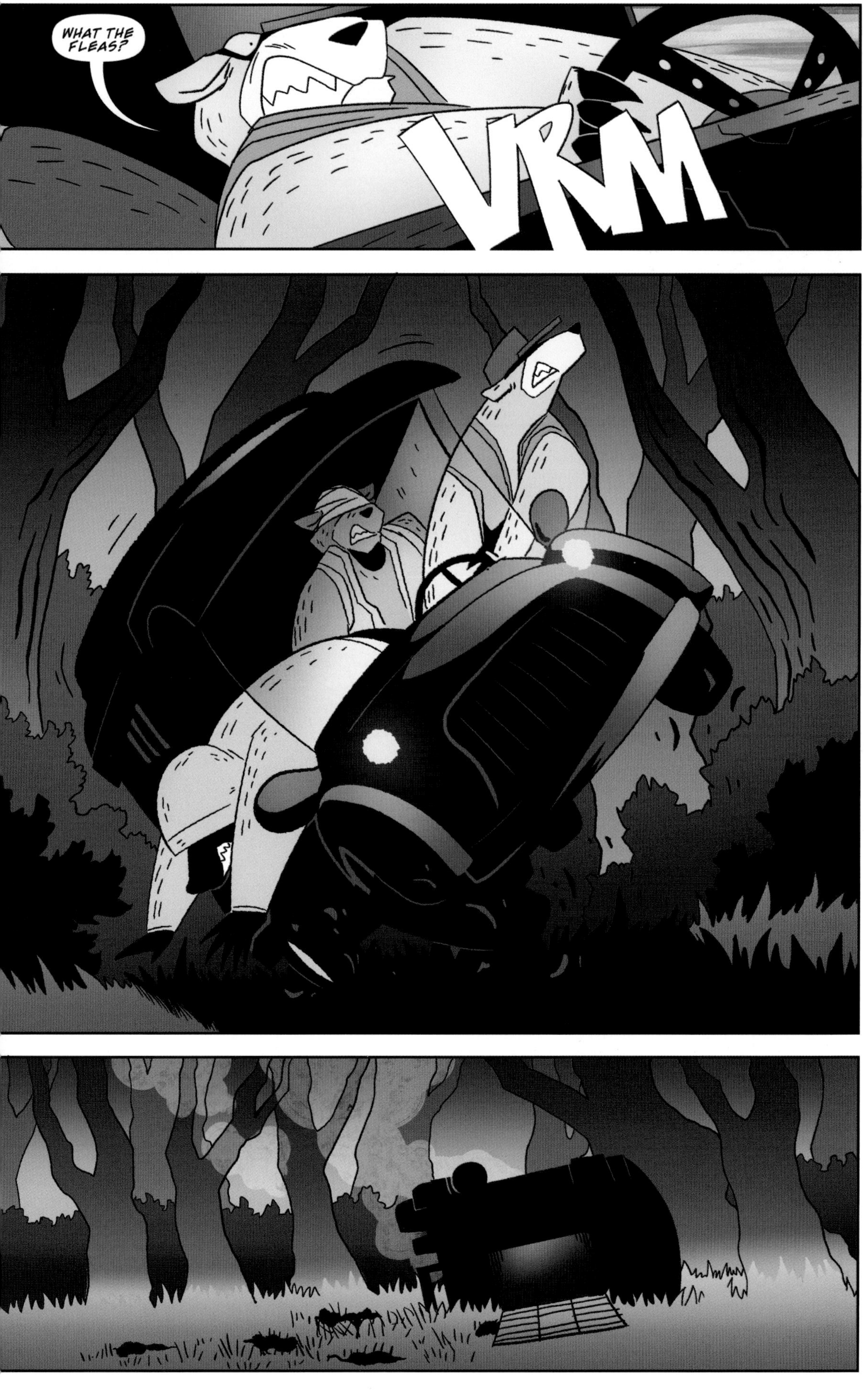
WHAT THE FLEAS?
VRM

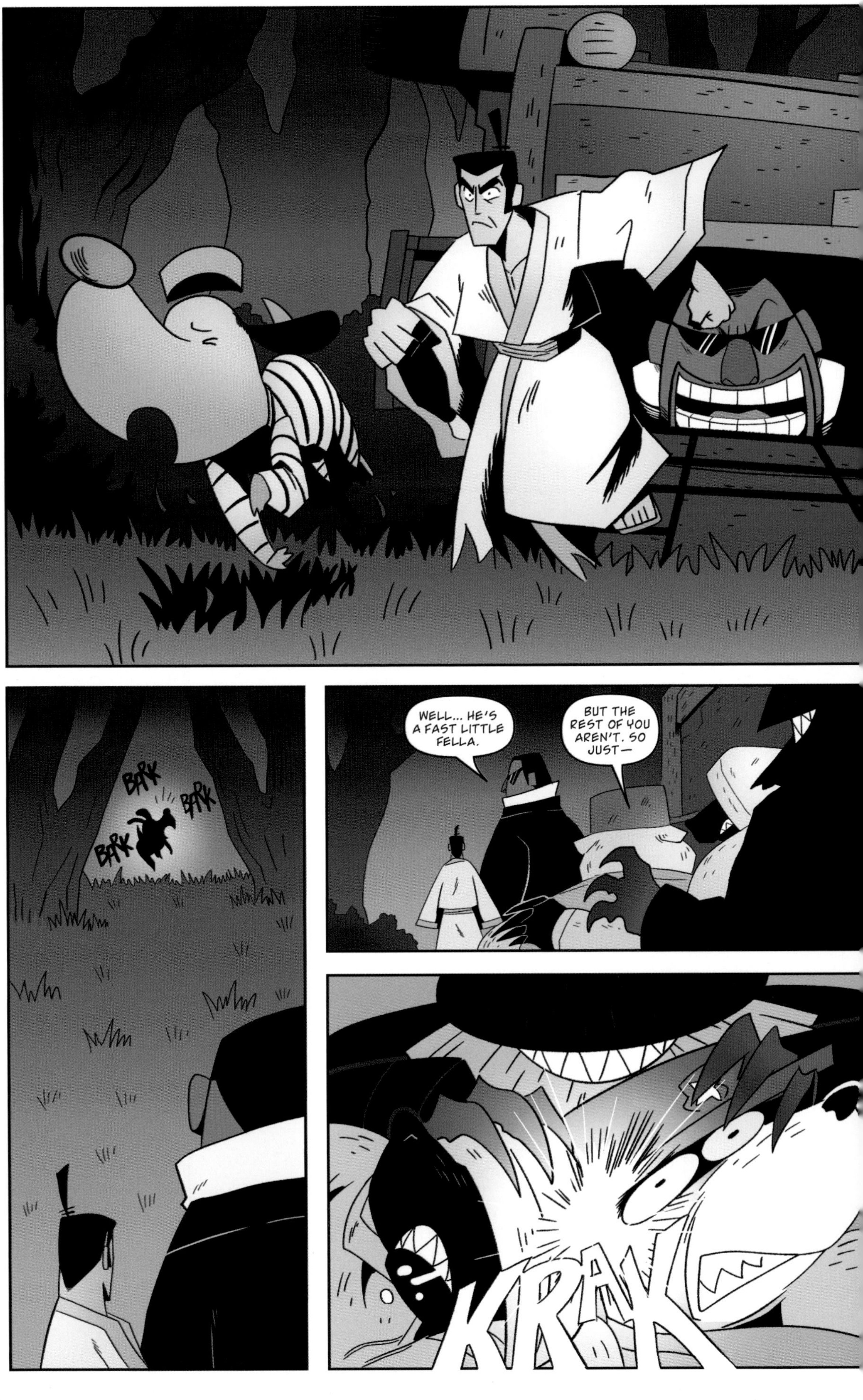
BARK
BARK
BARK
WELL... HE'S A FAST LITTLE FELLA.
BUT THE REST OF YOU AREN'T. SO JUST—
KRAK

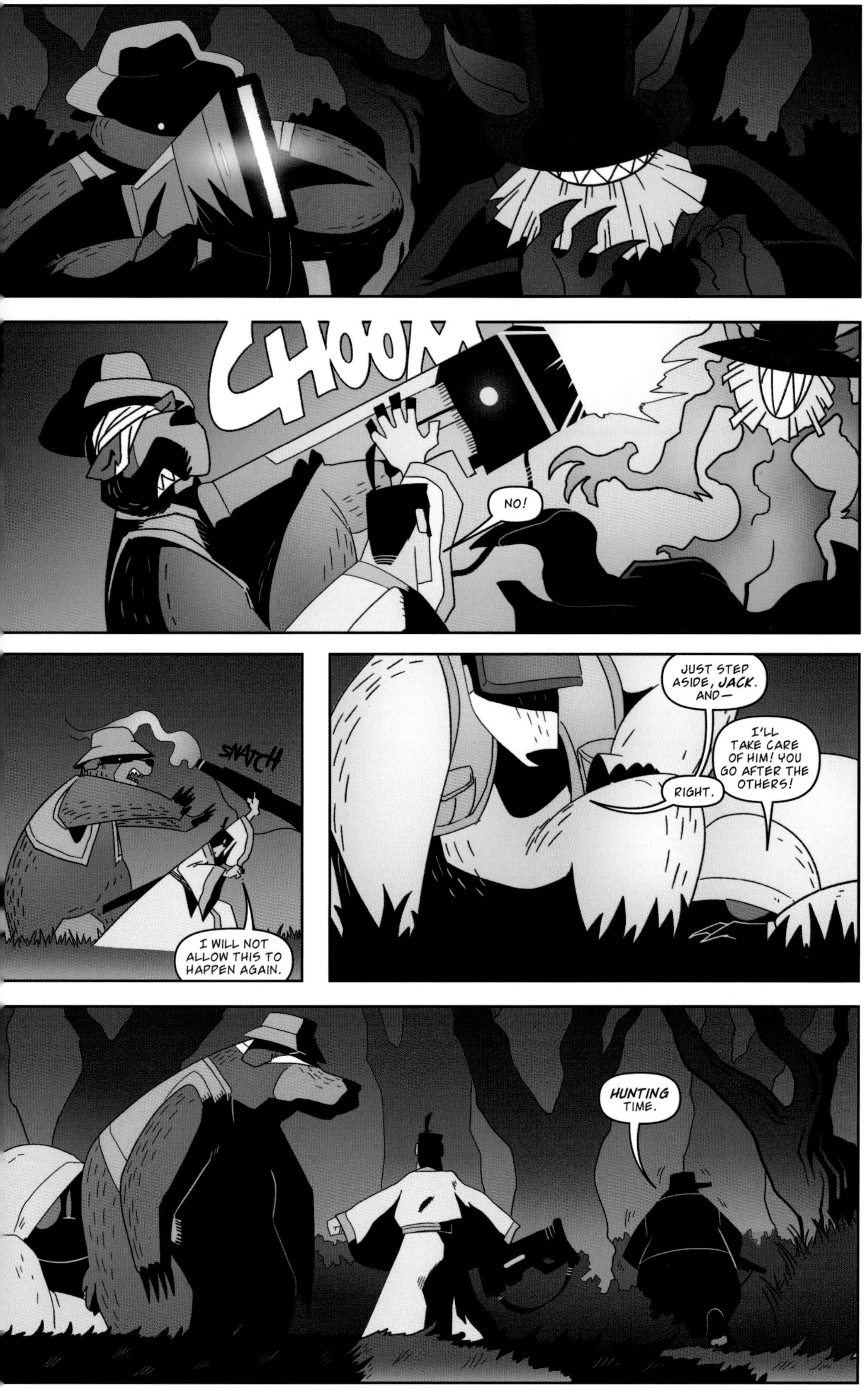
CHOOM
NO!
SNATCH
I WILL NOT ALLOW THIS TO HAPPEN AGAIN.
JUST STEP ASIDE, JACK. AND—
I'LL TAKE CARE OF HIM! YOU GO AFTER THE OTHERS!
RIGHT.
HUNTING TIME.

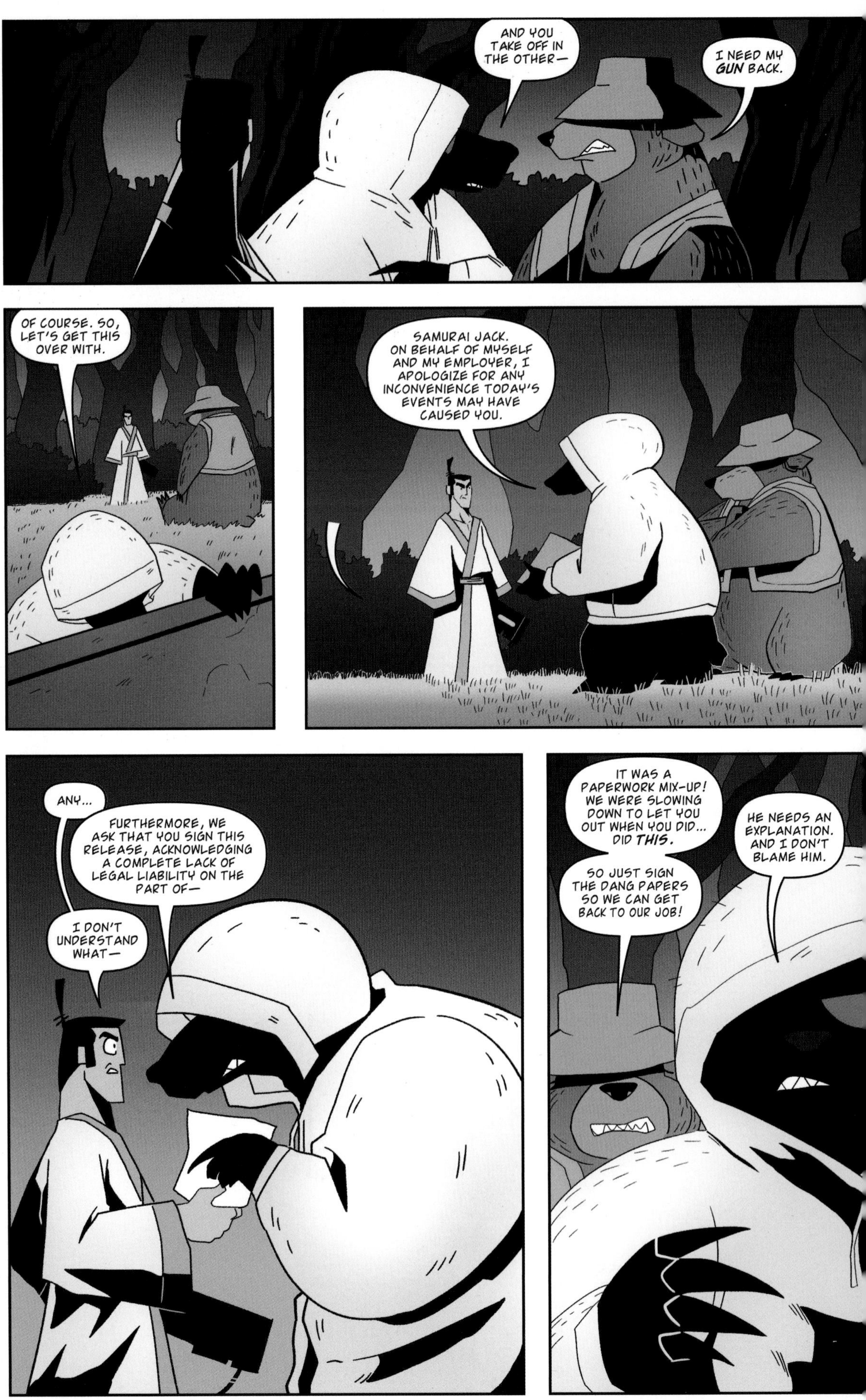
AND YOU TAKE OFF IN THE OTHER—
I NEED MY **GUN** BACK.
OF COURSE. SO, LET'S GET THIS OVER WITH.
SAMURAI JACK. ON BEHALF OF MYSELF AND MY EMPLOYER, I APOLOGIZE FOR ANY INCONVENIENCE TODAY'S EVENTS MAY HAVE CAUSED YOU.
ANY...
FURTHERMORE, WE ASK THAT YOU SIGN THIS RELEASE, ACKNOWLEDGING A COMPLETE LACK OF LEGAL LIABILITY ON THE PART OF—
I DON'T UNDERSTAND WHAT—
IT WAS A PAPERWORK MIX-UP! WE WERE SLOWING DOWN TO LET YOU OUT WHEN YOU DID... DID **THIS.**
SO JUST SIGN THE DANG PAPERS SO WE CAN GET BACK TO OUR JOB!
HE NEEDS AN EXPLANATION. AND I DON'T BLAME HIM.

OUR JOB IS TO TRACK DOWN THOSE INDIVIDUALS WHO HAVE... *EVADED* DEATH, WHETHER THROUGH MAGIC OR SOME OTHER MEANS.

FUGITIVES FROM THE *UNDERWORLD*.

AND WE THOUGHT YOU WERE OUR QUARRY. BECAUSE... WELL...

APPARENTLY, YOU'VE BEEN AROUND A VERY, VERY LONG TIME.

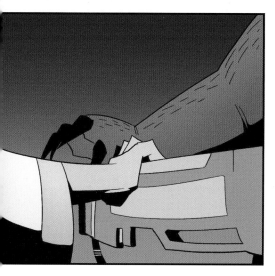

WAIT.

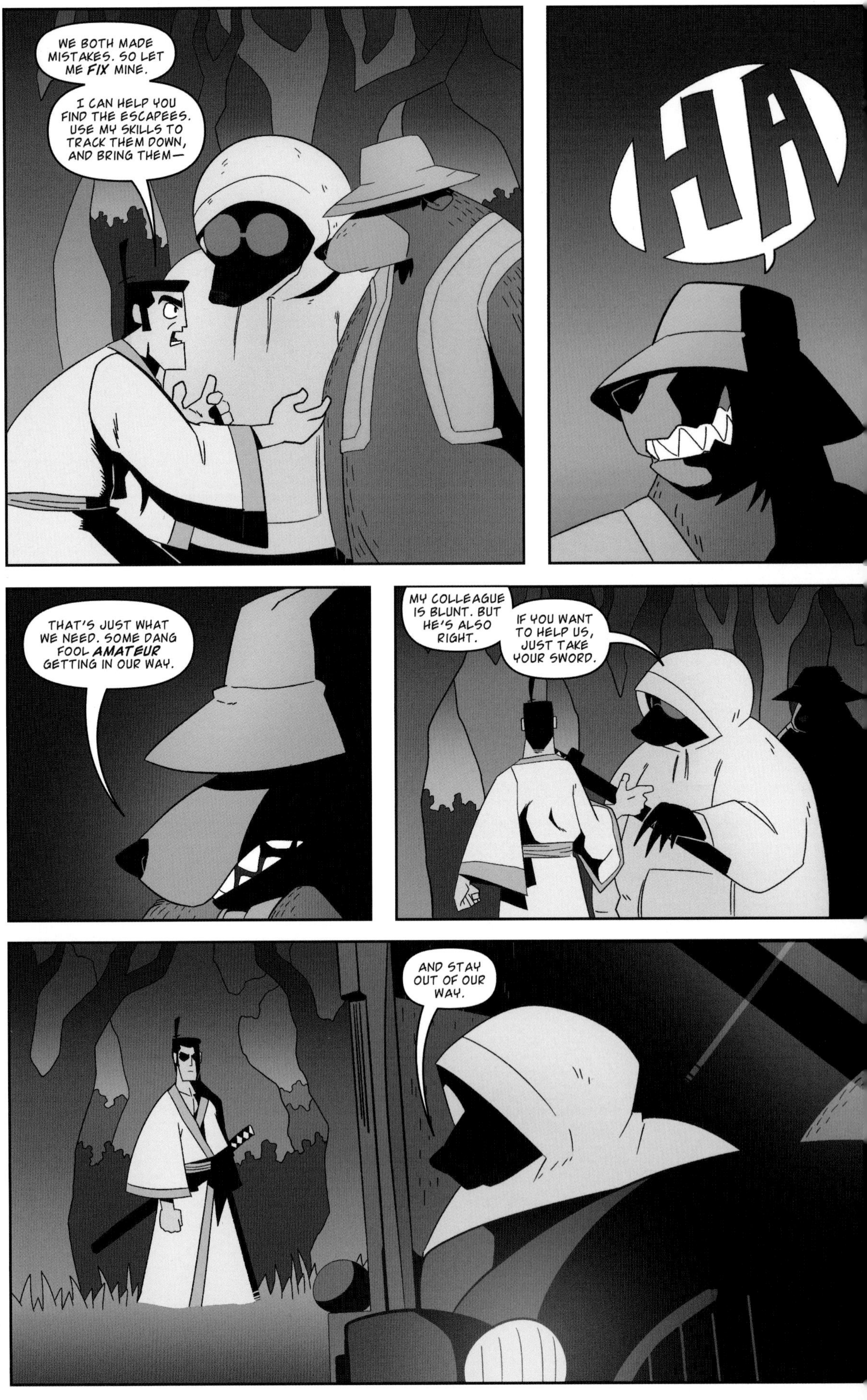
WE BOTH MADE MISTAKES. SO LET ME FIX MINE.
I CAN HELP YOU FIND THE ESCAPEES. USE MY SKILLS TO TRACK THEM DOWN, AND BRING THEM—
THAT'S JUST WHAT WE NEED. SOME DANG FOOL AMATEUR GETTING IN OUR WAY.
MY COLLEAGUE IS BLUNT. BUT HE'S ALSO RIGHT.
IF YOU WANT TO HELP US, JUST TAKE YOUR SWORD.
AND STAY OUT OF OUR WAY.

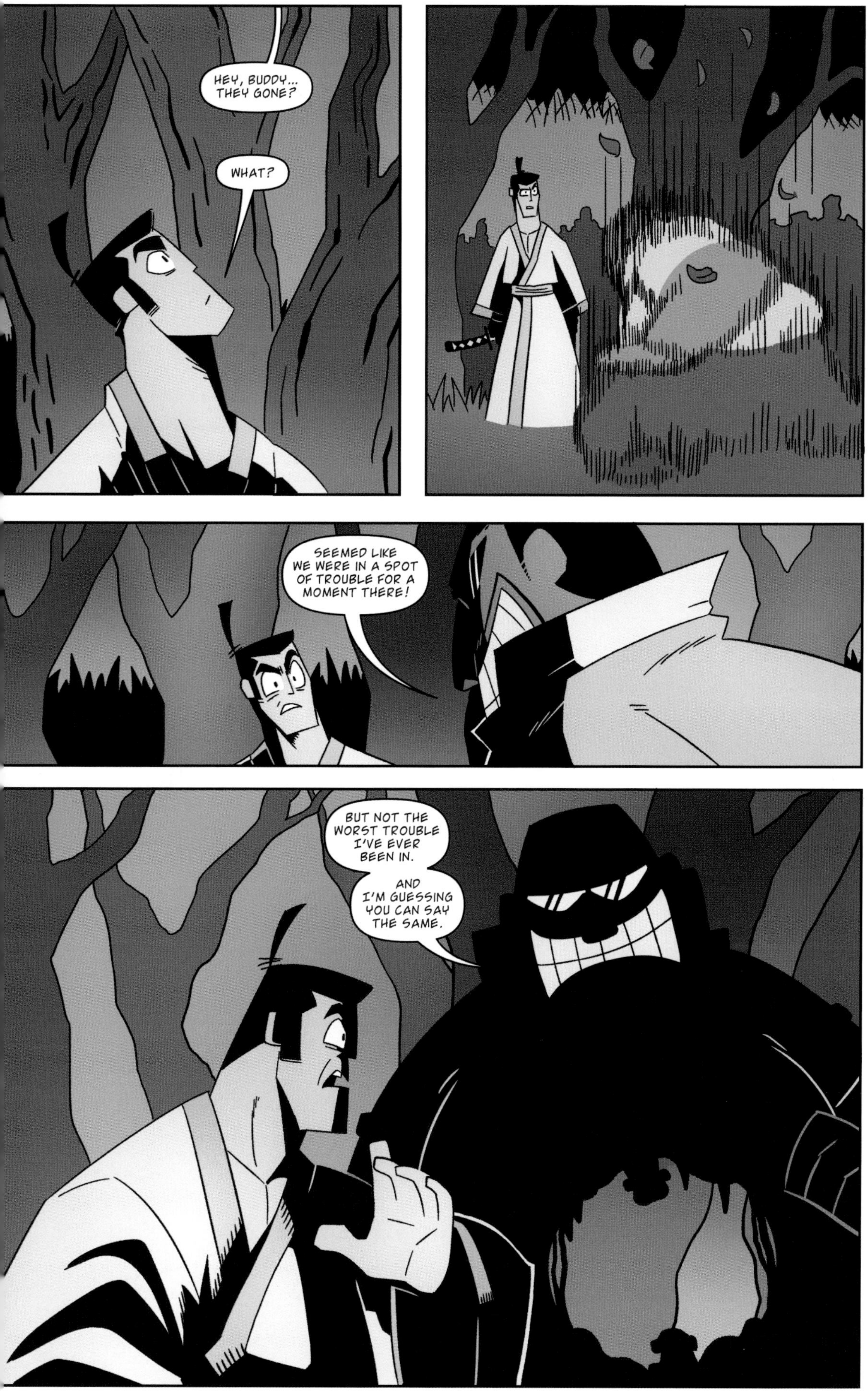
HEY, BUDDY... THEY GONE?
WHAT?
SEEMED LIKE WE WERE IN A SPOT OF TROUBLE FOR A MOMENT THERE!
BUT NOT THE WORST TROUBLE I'VE EVER BEEN IN.
AND I'M GUESSING YOU CAN SAY THE SAME.

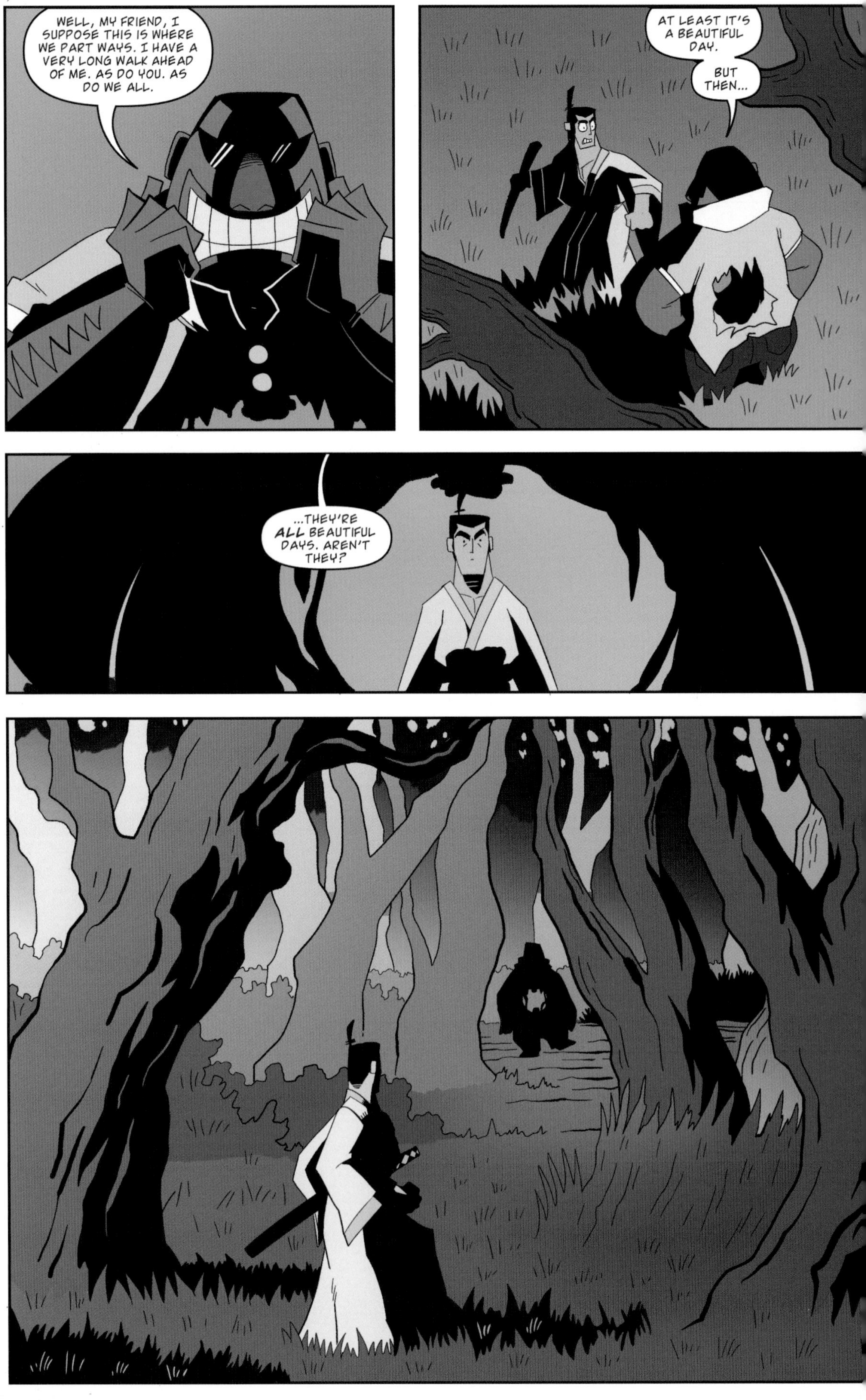
WELL, MY FRIEND, I SUPPOSE THIS IS WHERE WE PART WAYS. I HAVE A VERY LONG WALK AHEAD OF ME. AS DO YOU. AS DO WE ALL.
AT LEAST IT'S A BEAUTIFUL DAY.
BUT THEN...
...THEY'RE ALL BEAUTIFUL DAYS. AREN'T THEY?

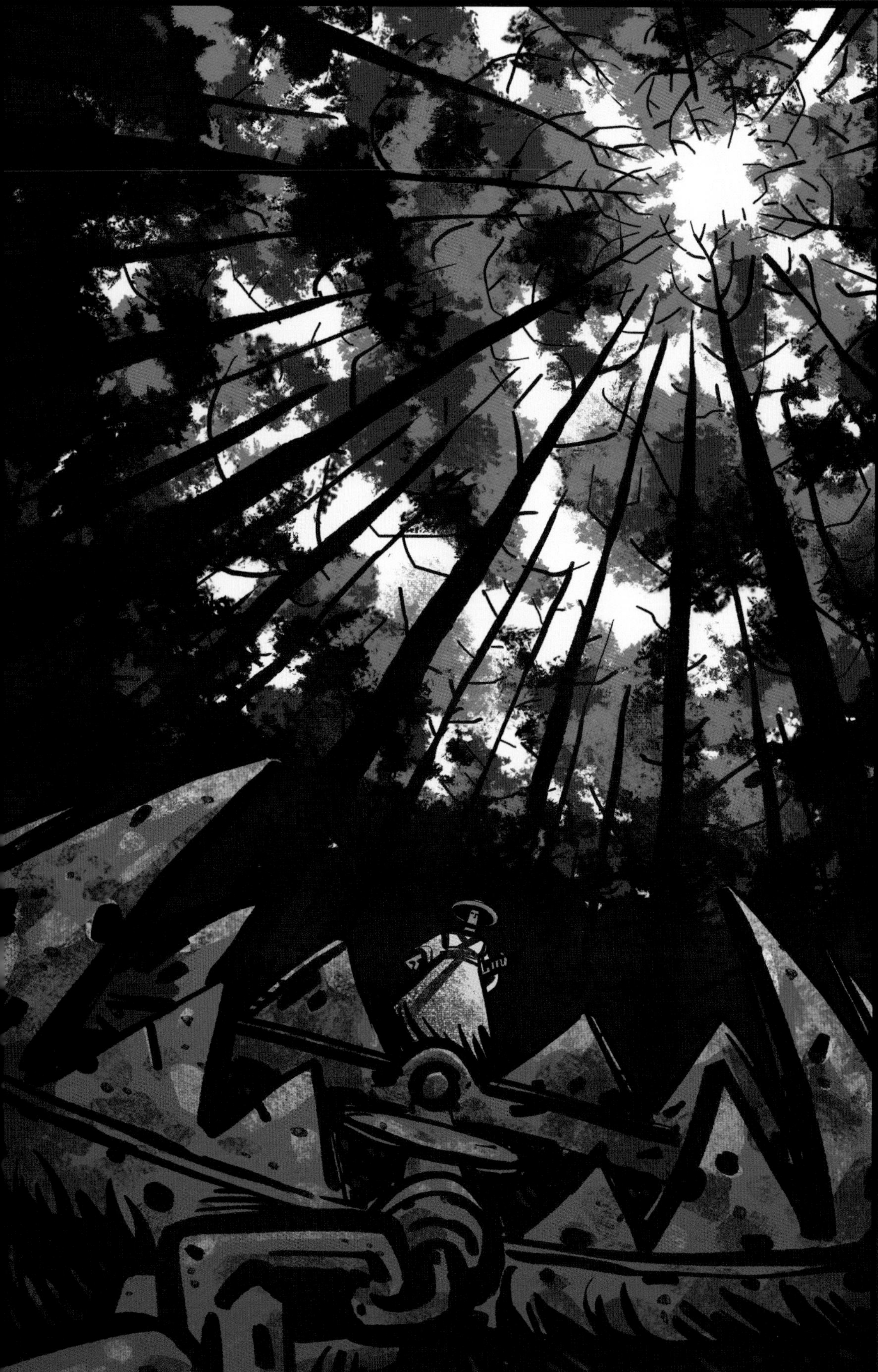

Art by Gavin Fullerton

Art by Adam Bryce Thomas

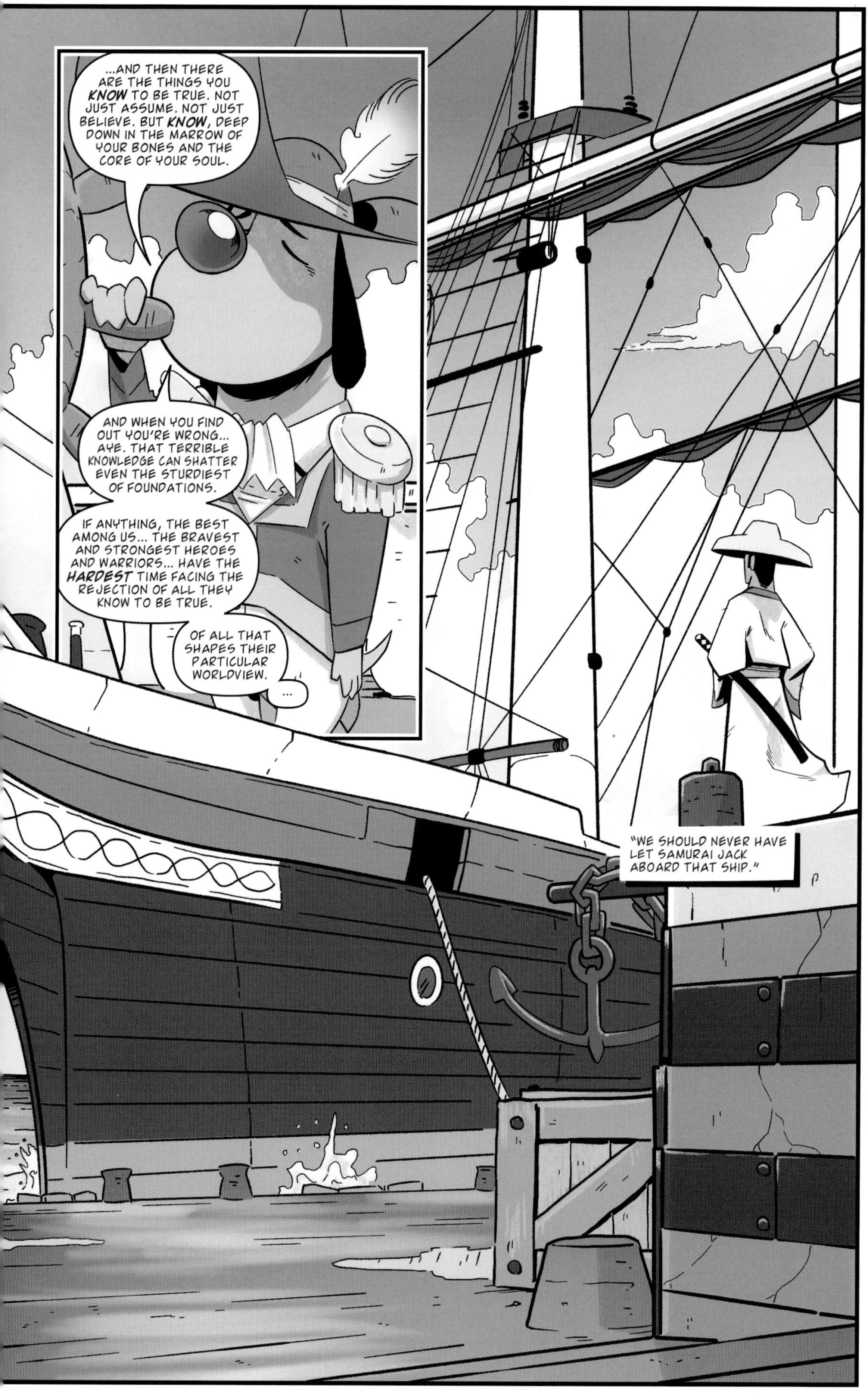
...AND THEN THERE ARE THE THINGS YOU KNOW TO BE TRUE. NOT JUST ASSUME. NOT JUST BELIEVE. BUT KNOW, DEEP DOWN IN THE MARROW OF YOUR BONES AND THE CORE OF YOUR SOUL.
AND WHEN YOU FIND OUT YOU'RE WRONG... AYE. THAT TERRIBLE KNOWLEDGE CAN SHATTER EVEN THE STURDIEST OF FOUNDATIONS.
IF ANYTHING, THE BEST AMONG US... THE BRAVEST AND STRONGEST HEROES AND WARRIORS... HAVE THE HARDEST TIME FACING THE REJECTION OF ALL THEY KNOW TO BE TRUE.
OF ALL THAT SHAPES THEIR PARTICULAR WORLDVIEW.
...
"WE SHOULD NEVER HAVE LET SAMURAI JACK ABOARD THAT SHIP."

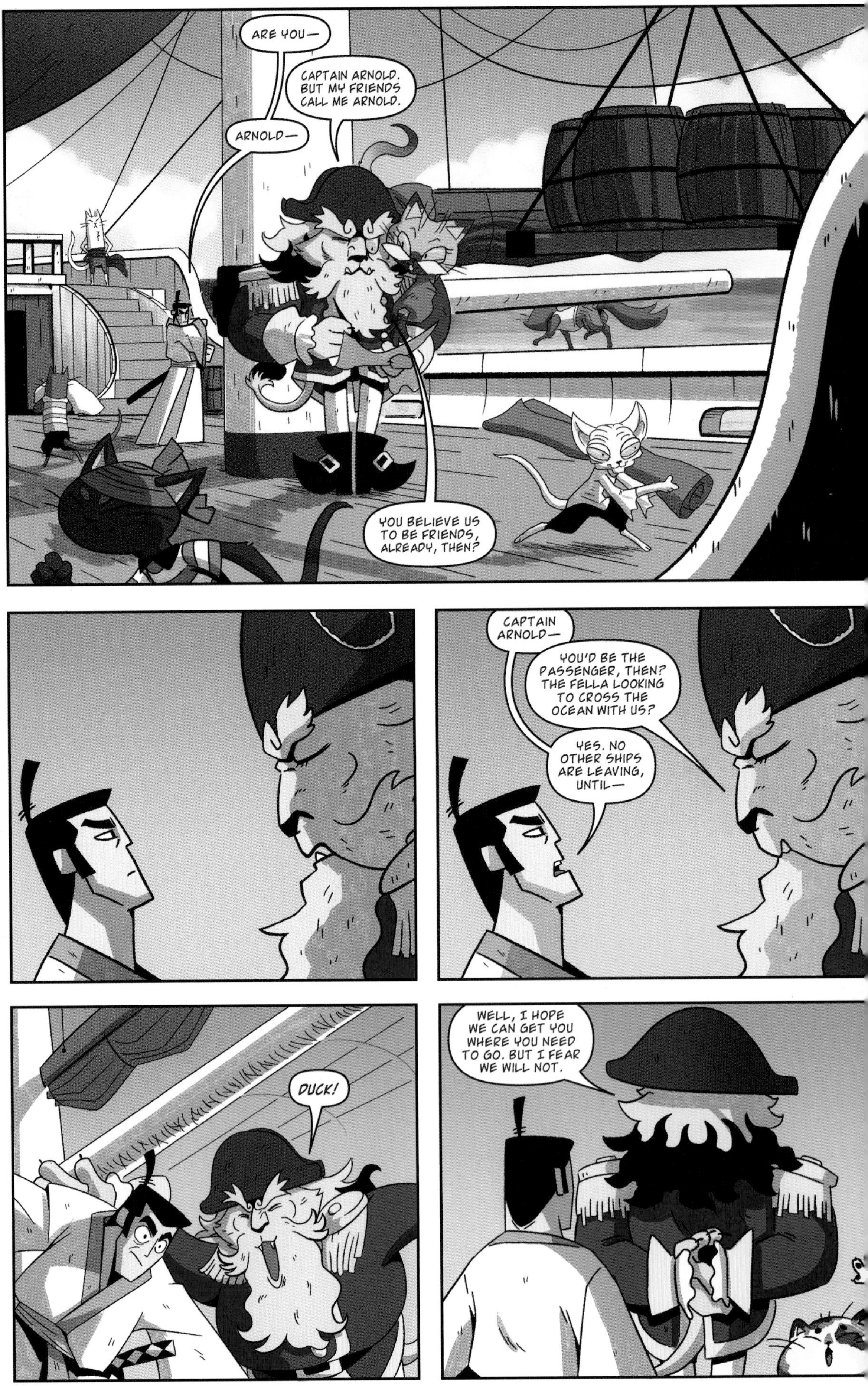
ARE YOU—
CAPTAIN ARNOLD. BUT MY FRIENDS CALL ME ARNOLD.
ARNOLD—
YOU BELIEVE US TO BE FRIENDS, ALREADY, THEN?
CAPTAIN ARNOLD—
YOU'D BE THE PASSENGER, THEN? THE FELLA LOOKING TO CROSS THE OCEAN WITH US?
YES. NO OTHER SHIPS ARE LEAVING, UNTIL—
DUCK!
WELL, I HOPE WE CAN GET YOU WHERE YOU NEED TO GO. BUT I FEAR WE WILL NOT.

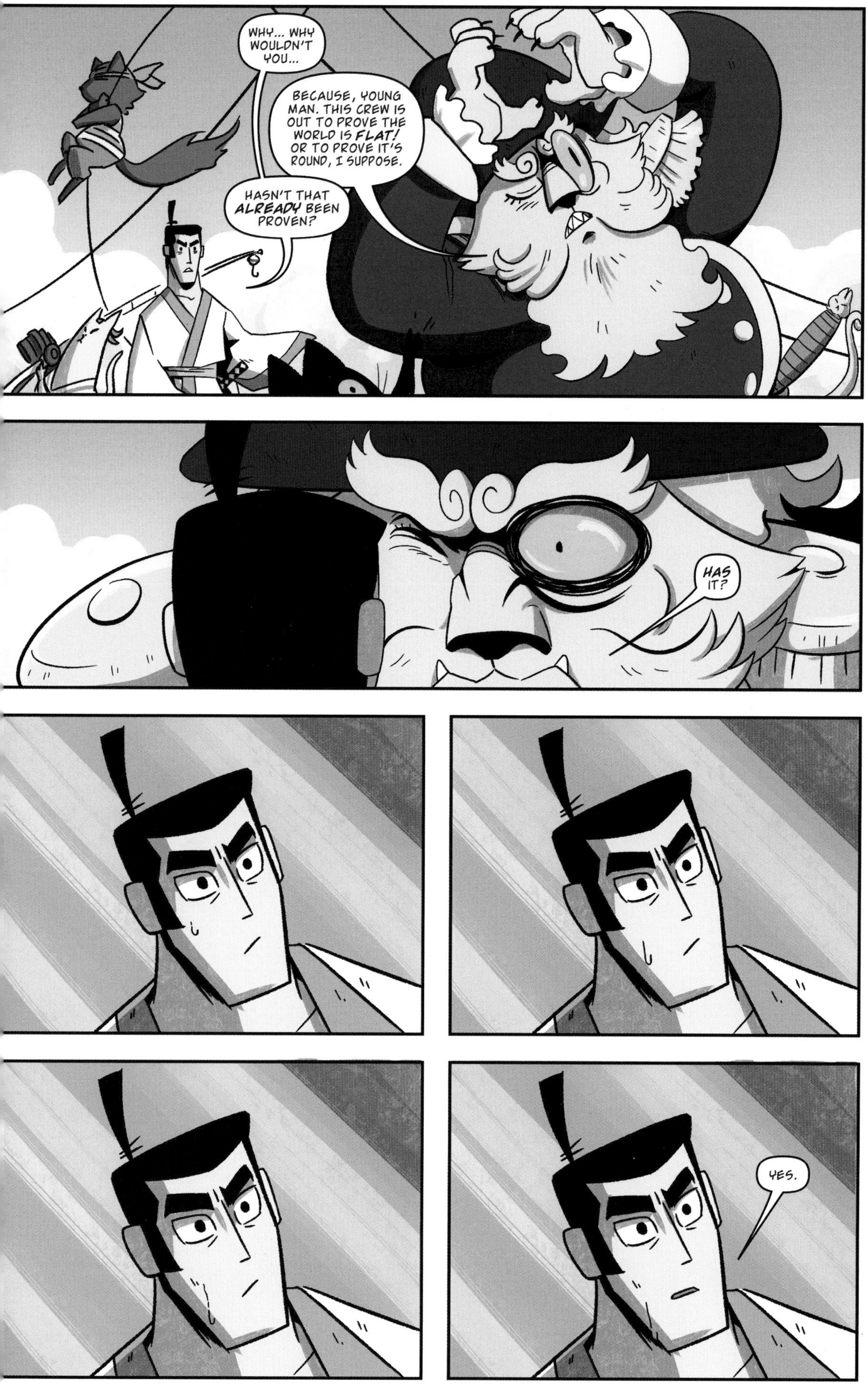
WHY... WHY WOULDN'T YOU...
BECAUSE, YOUNG MAN. THIS CREW IS OUT TO PROVE THE WORLD IS FLAT! OR TO PROVE IT'S ROUND, I SUPPOSE.
HASN'T THAT ALREADY BEEN PROVEN?
HAS IT?
YES.

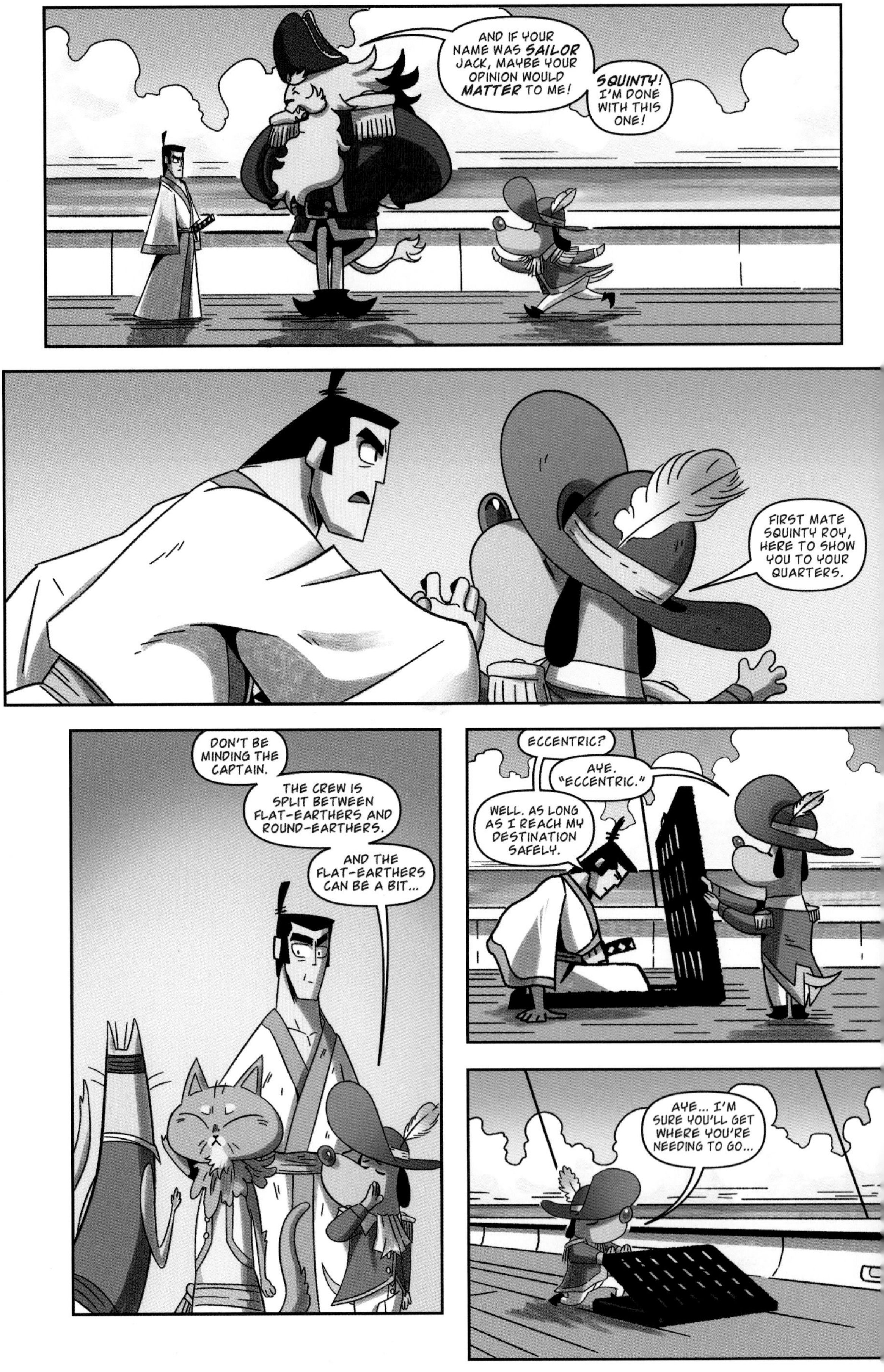

AND IF YOUR NAME WAS SAILOR JACK, MAYBE YOUR OPINION WOULD MATTER TO ME!
SQUINTY! I'M DONE WITH THIS ONE!
FIRST MATE SQUINTY ROY, HERE TO SHOW YOU TO YOUR QUARTERS.
DON'T BE MINDING THE CAPTAIN.
THE CREW IS SPLIT BETWEEN FLAT-EARTHERS AND ROUND-EARTHERS.
AND THE FLAT-EARTHERS CAN BE A BIT...
ECCENTRIC?
AYE. "ECCENTRIC."
WELL. AS LONG AS I REACH MY DESTINATION SAFELY.
AYE... I'M SURE YOU'LL GET WHERE YOU'RE NEEDING TO GO...

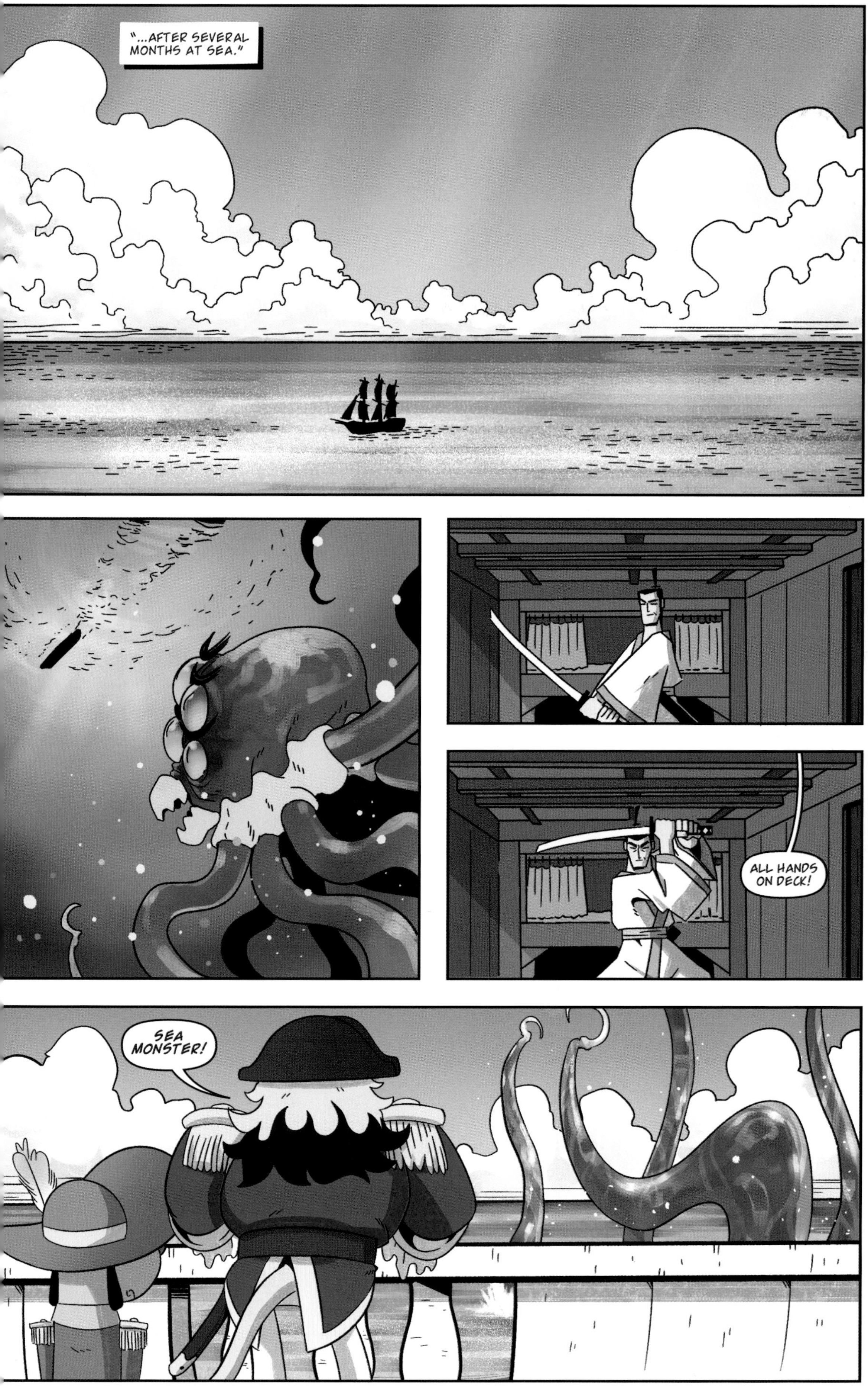
"...AFTER SEVERAL MONTHS AT SEA."
ALL HANDS ON DECK!
SEA MONSTER!

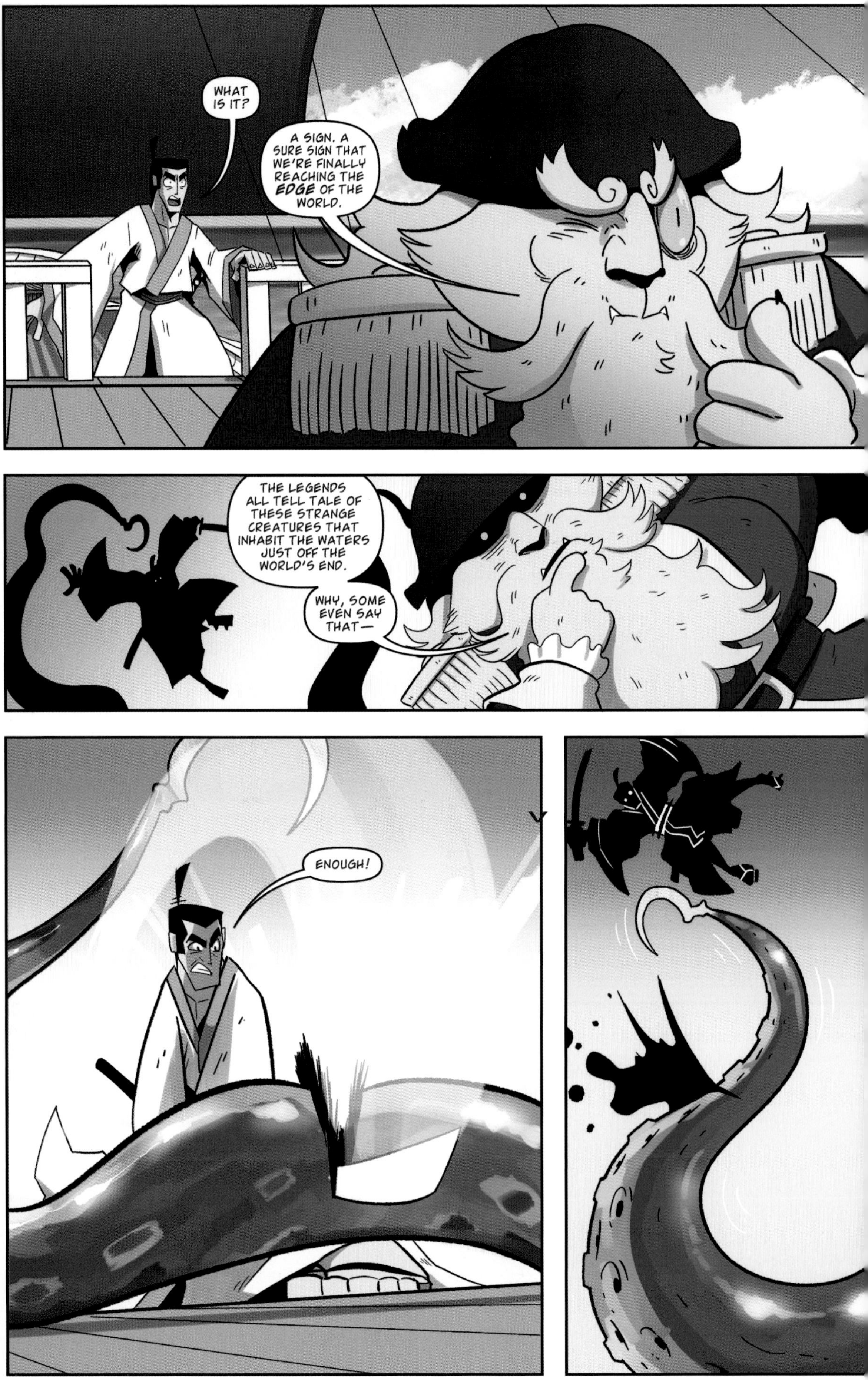
WHAT IS IT?
A SIGN. A SURE SIGN THAT WE'RE FINALLY REACHING THE **EDGE** OF THE WORLD.
THE LEGENDS ALL TELL TALE OF THESE STRANGE CREATURES THAT INHABIT THE WATERS JUST OFF THE WORLD'S END.
WHY, SOME EVEN SAY THAT—
ENOUGH!

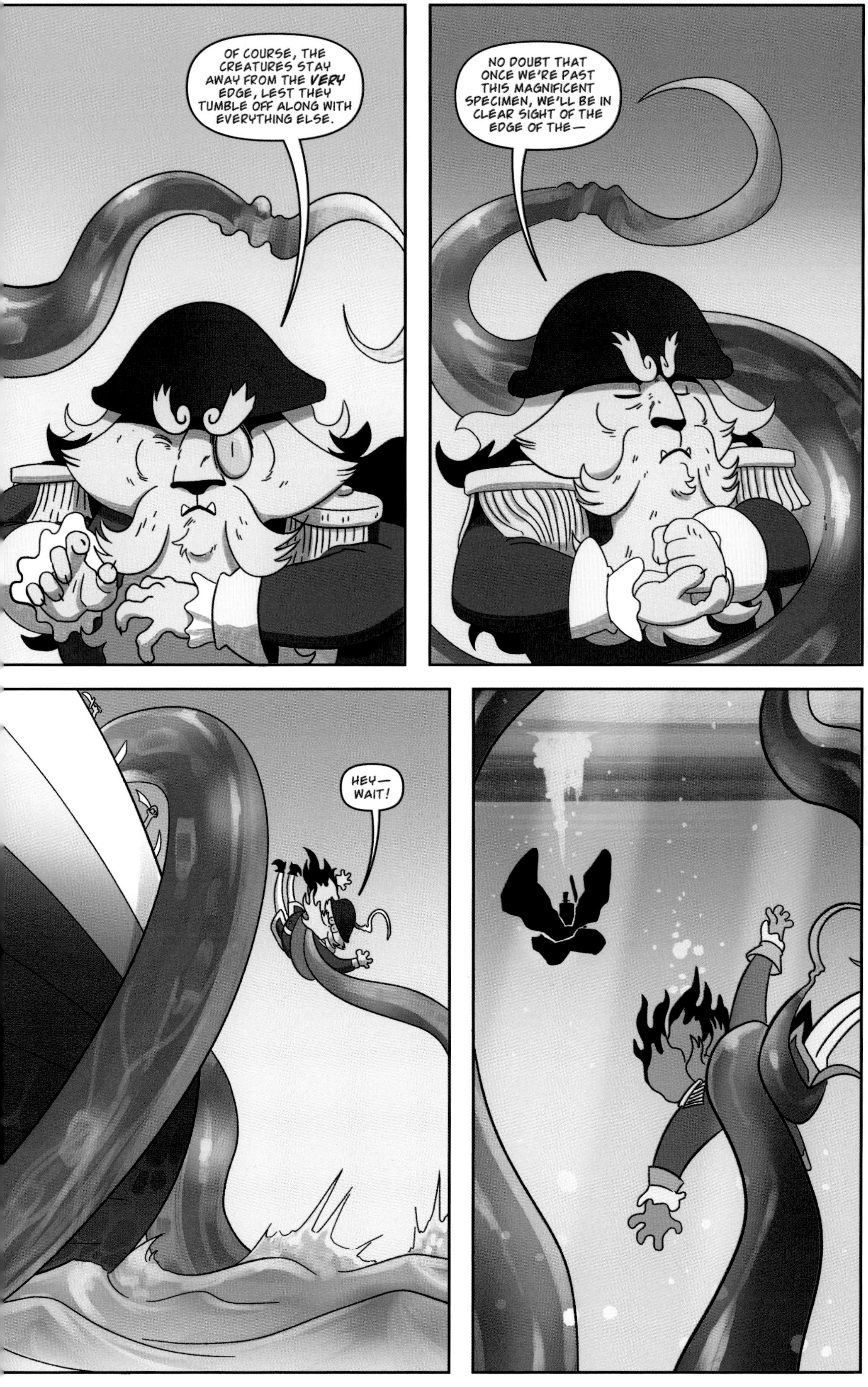
OF COURSE, THE CREATURES STAY AWAY FROM THE VERY EDGE, LEST THEY TUMBLE OFF ALONG WITH EVERYTHING ELSE.
NO DOUBT THAT ONCE WE'RE PAST THIS MAGNIFICENT SPECIMEN, WE'LL BE IN CLEAR SIGHT OF THE EDGE OF THE—
HEY— WAIT!

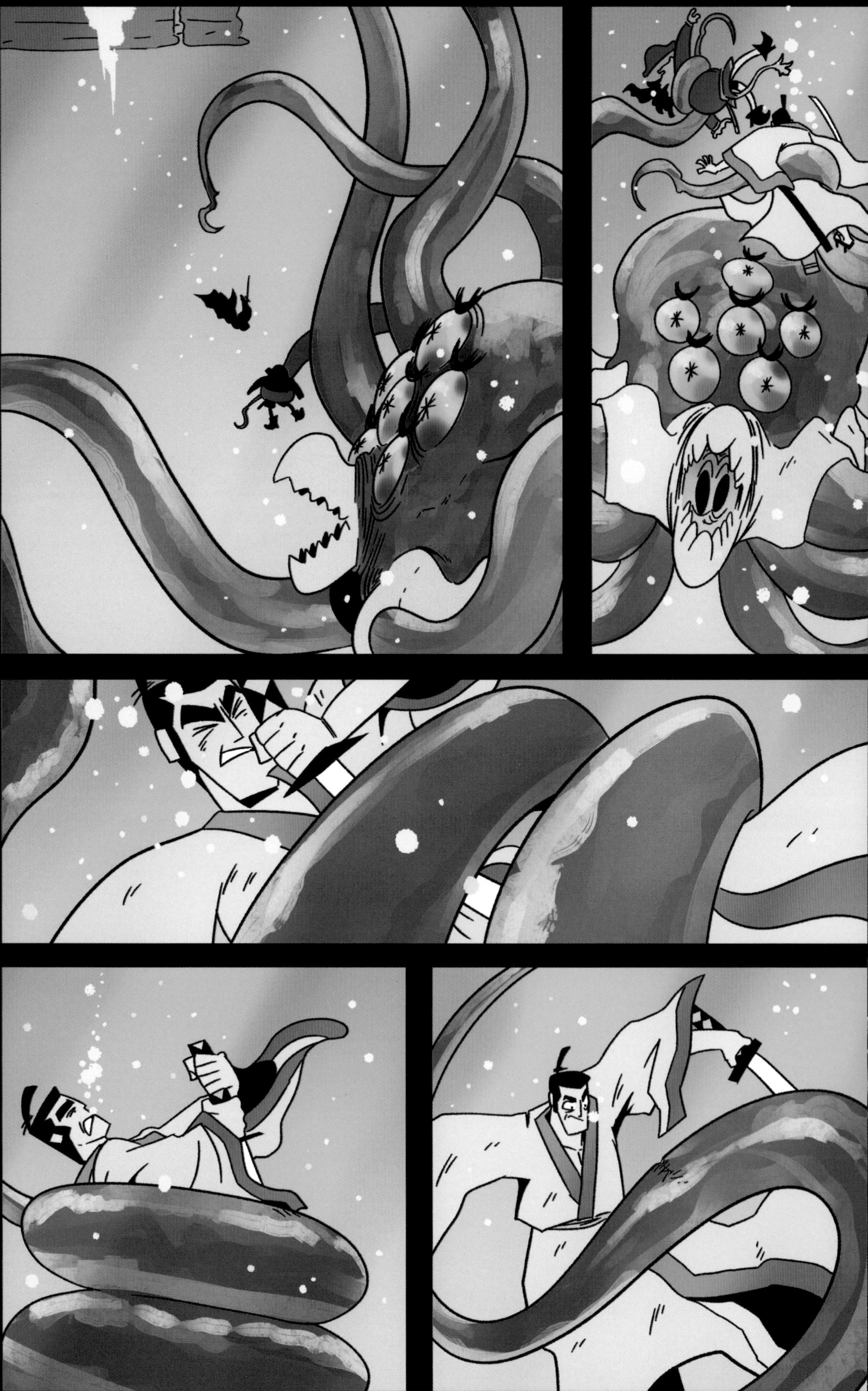

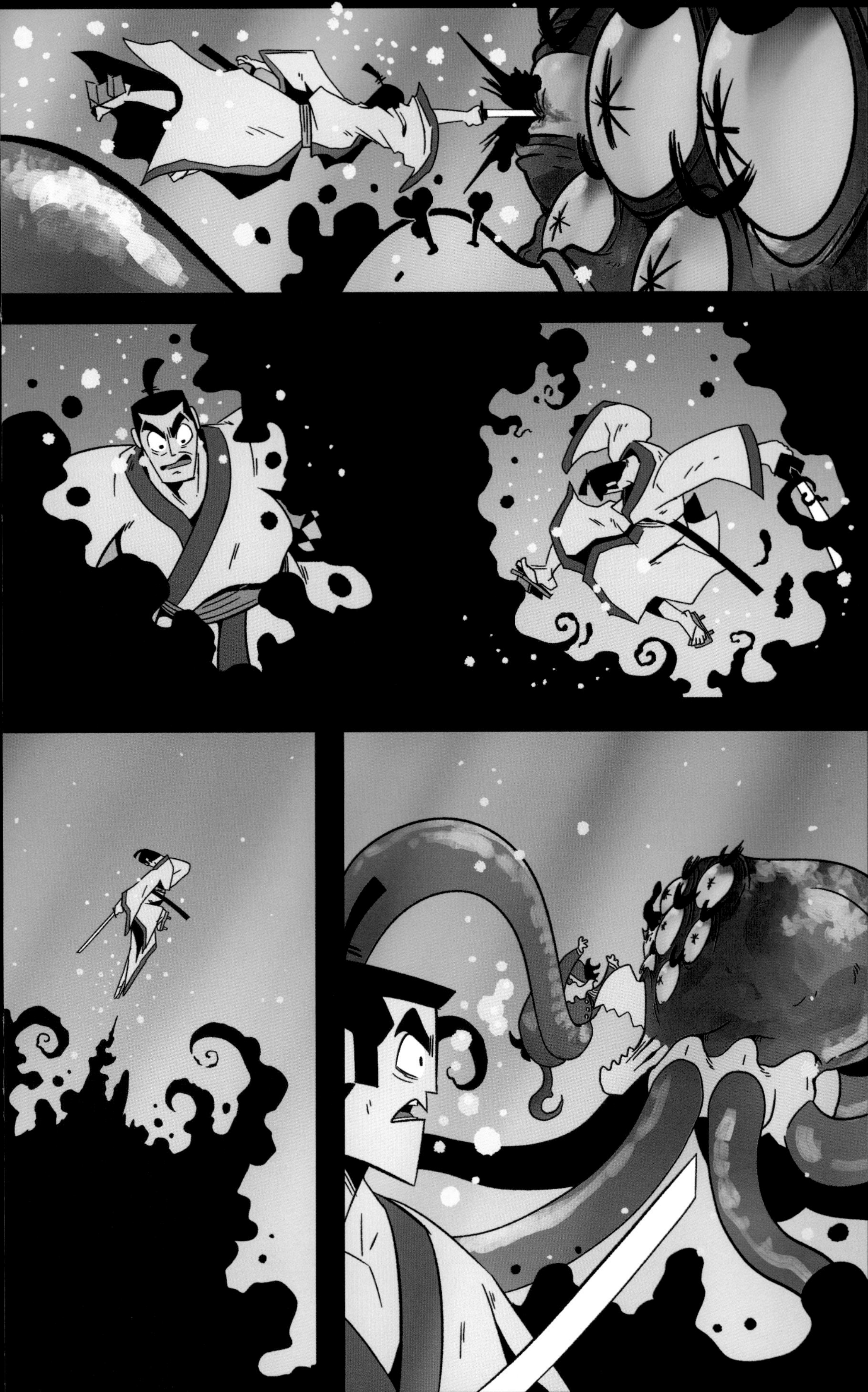

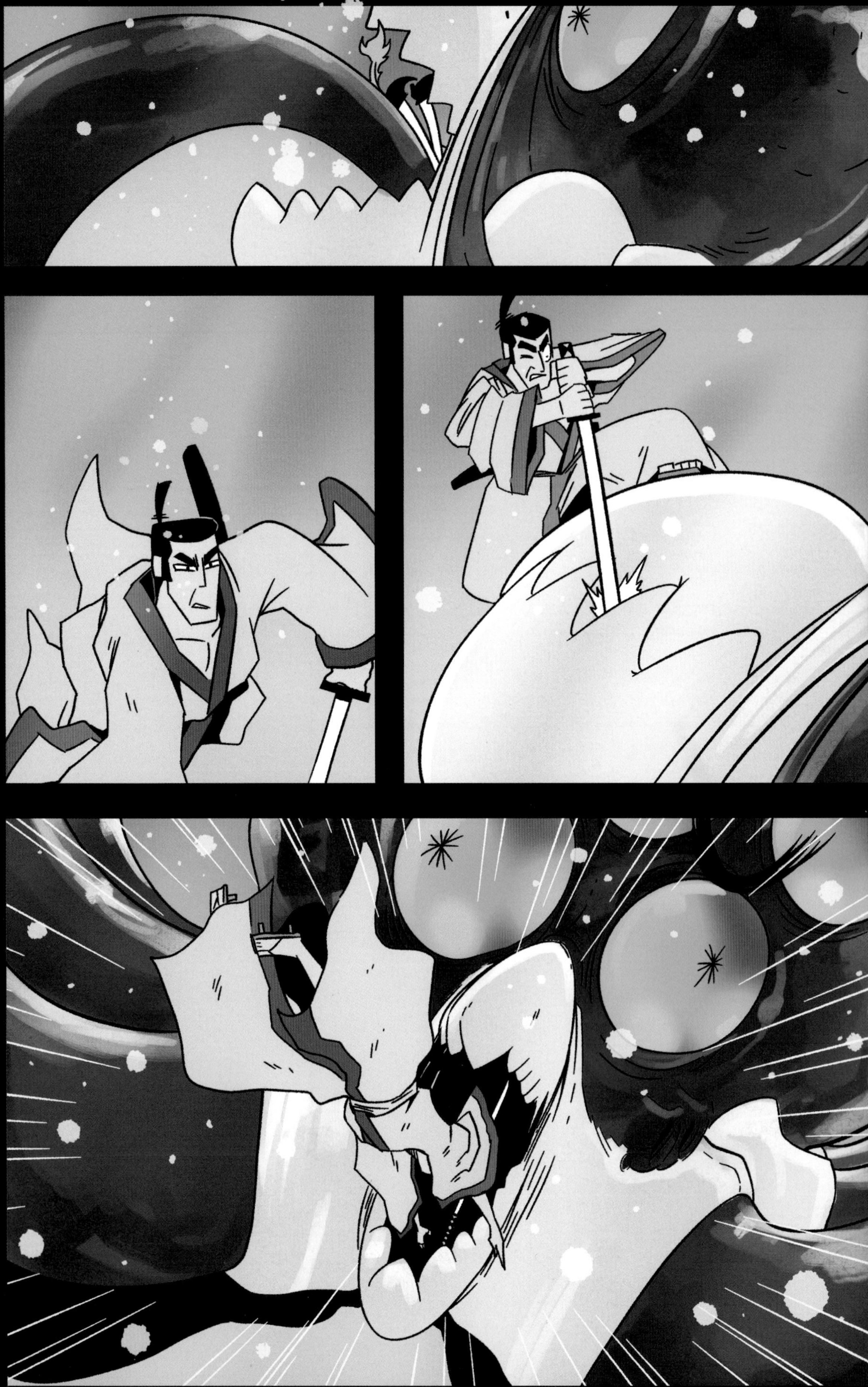

P-TWOO

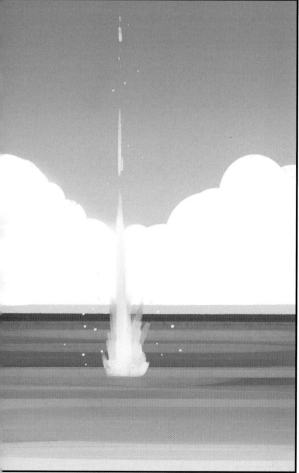

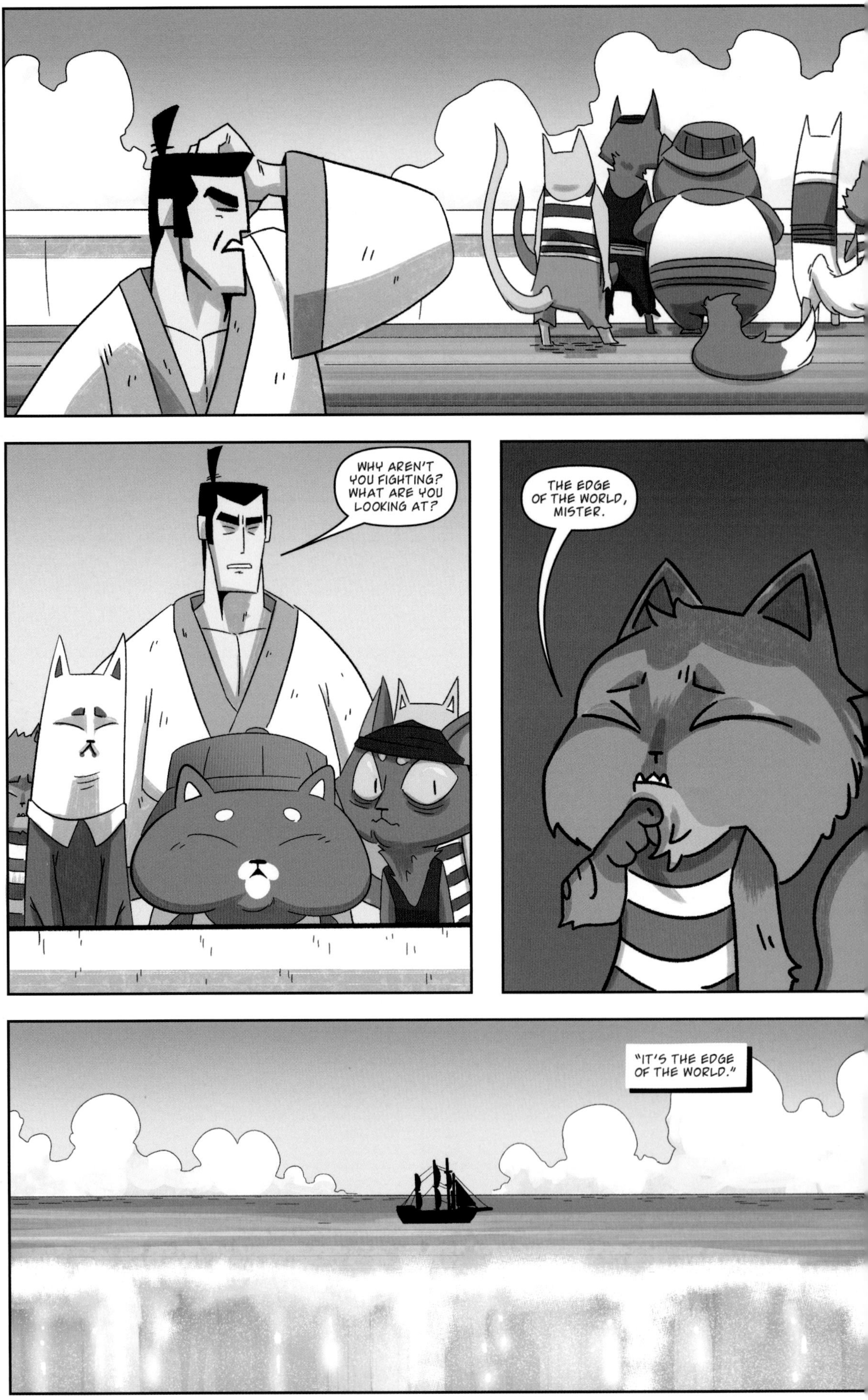
WHY AREN'T YOU FIGHTING? WHAT ARE YOU LOOKING AT?
THE EDGE OF THE WORLD, MISTER.
"IT'S THE EDGE OF THE WORLD."

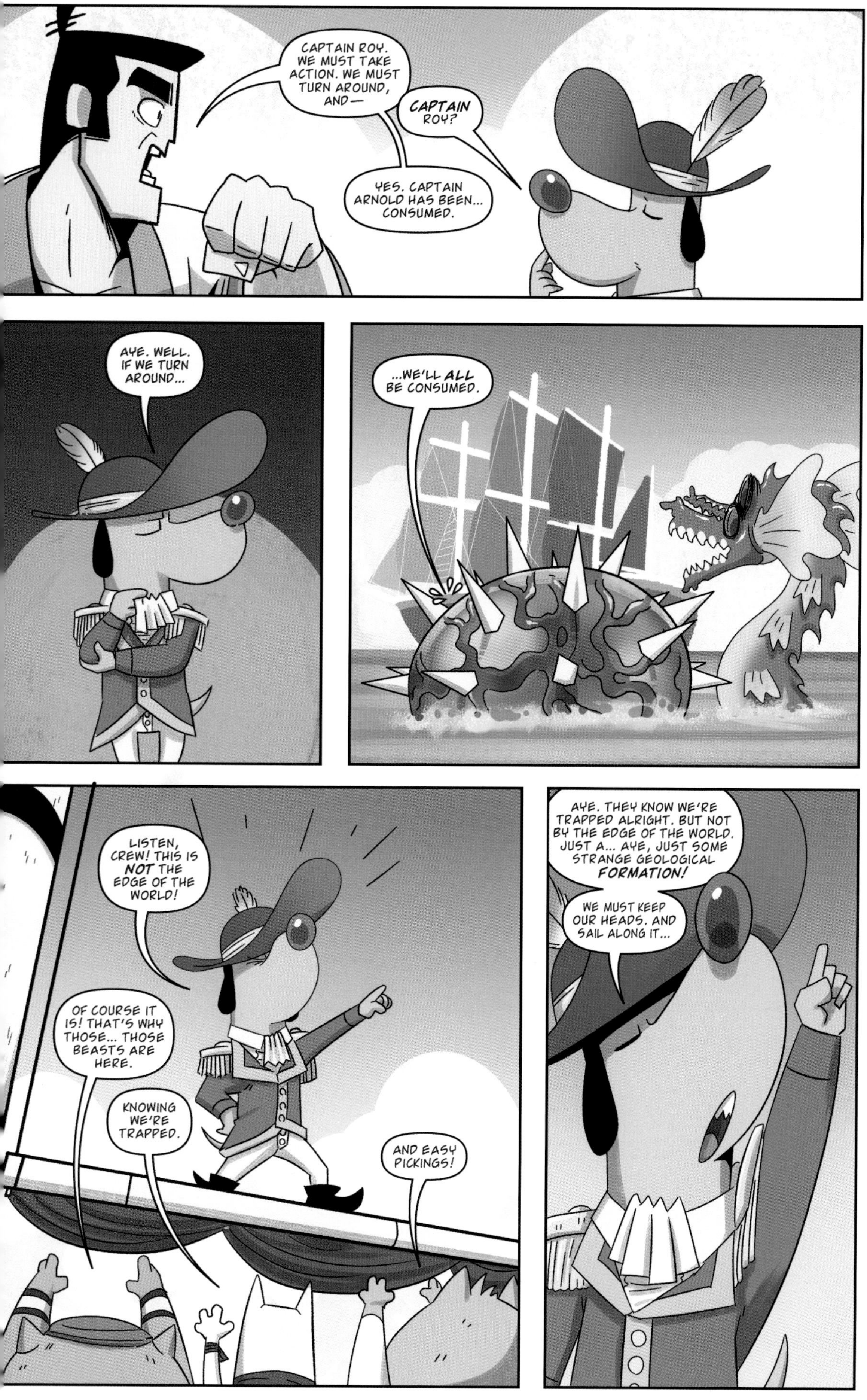
CAPTAIN ROY. WE MUST TAKE ACTION. WE MUST TURN AROUND, AND—
CAPTAIN ROY?
YES. CAPTAIN ARNOLD HAS BEEN... CONSUMED.
AYE. WELL. IF WE TURN AROUND...
...WE'LL ALL BE CONSUMED.
LISTEN, CREW! THIS IS NOT THE EDGE OF THE WORLD!
OF COURSE IT IS! THAT'S WHY THOSE... THOSE BEASTS ARE HERE.
KNOWING WE'RE TRAPPED.
AND EASY PICKINGS!
AYE. THEY KNOW WE'RE TRAPPED ALRIGHT. BUT NOT BY THE EDGE OF THE WORLD. JUST A... AYE, JUST SOME STRANGE GEOLOGICAL FORMATION!
WE MUST KEEP OUR HEADS. AND SAIL ALONG IT...

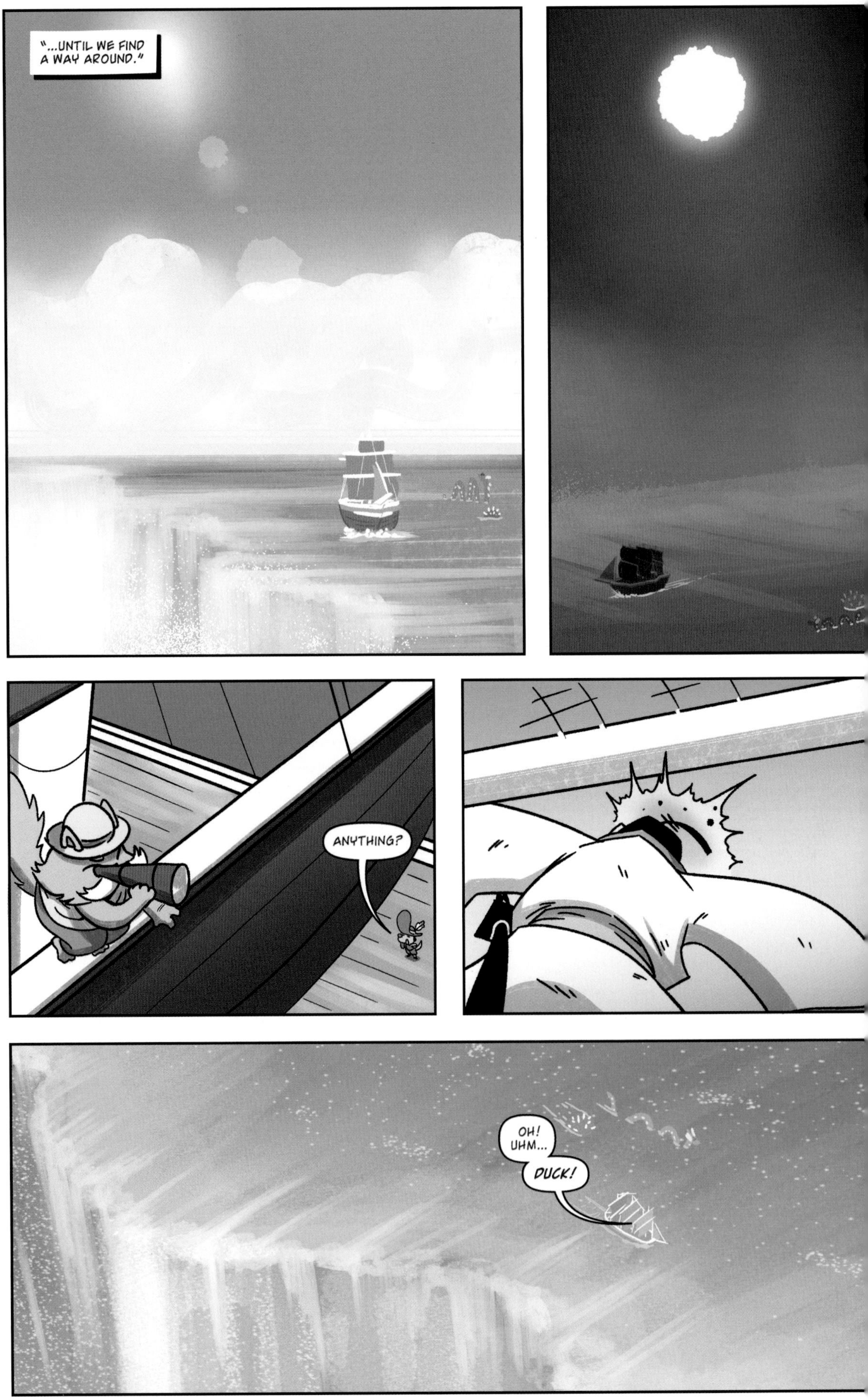
"...UNTIL WE FIND A WAY AROUND."
ANYTHING?
OH! UHM...
DUCK!

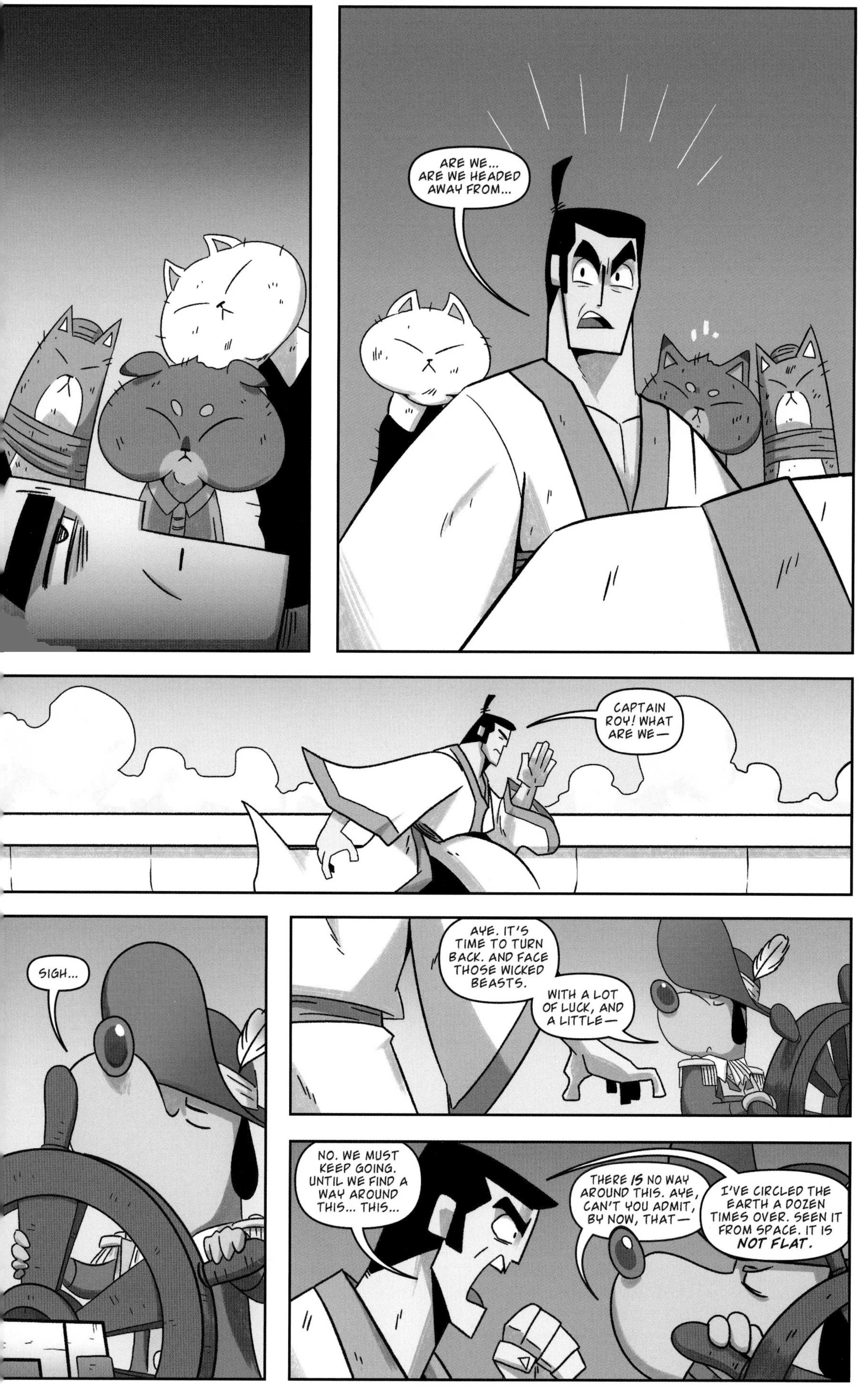
ARE WE... ARE WE HEADED AWAY FROM...
CAPTAIN ROY! WHAT ARE WE—
SIGH...
AYE. IT'S TIME TO TURN BACK. AND FACE THOSE WICKED BEASTS.
WITH A LOT OF LUCK, AND A LITTLE—
NO. WE MUST KEEP GOING. UNTIL WE FIND A WAY AROUND THIS... THIS...
THERE *IS* NO WAY AROUND THIS. AYE, CAN'T YOU ADMIT, BY NOW, THAT—
I'VE CIRCLED THE EARTH A DOZEN TIMES OVER. SEEN IT FROM SPACE. IT IS ***NOT FLAT***.

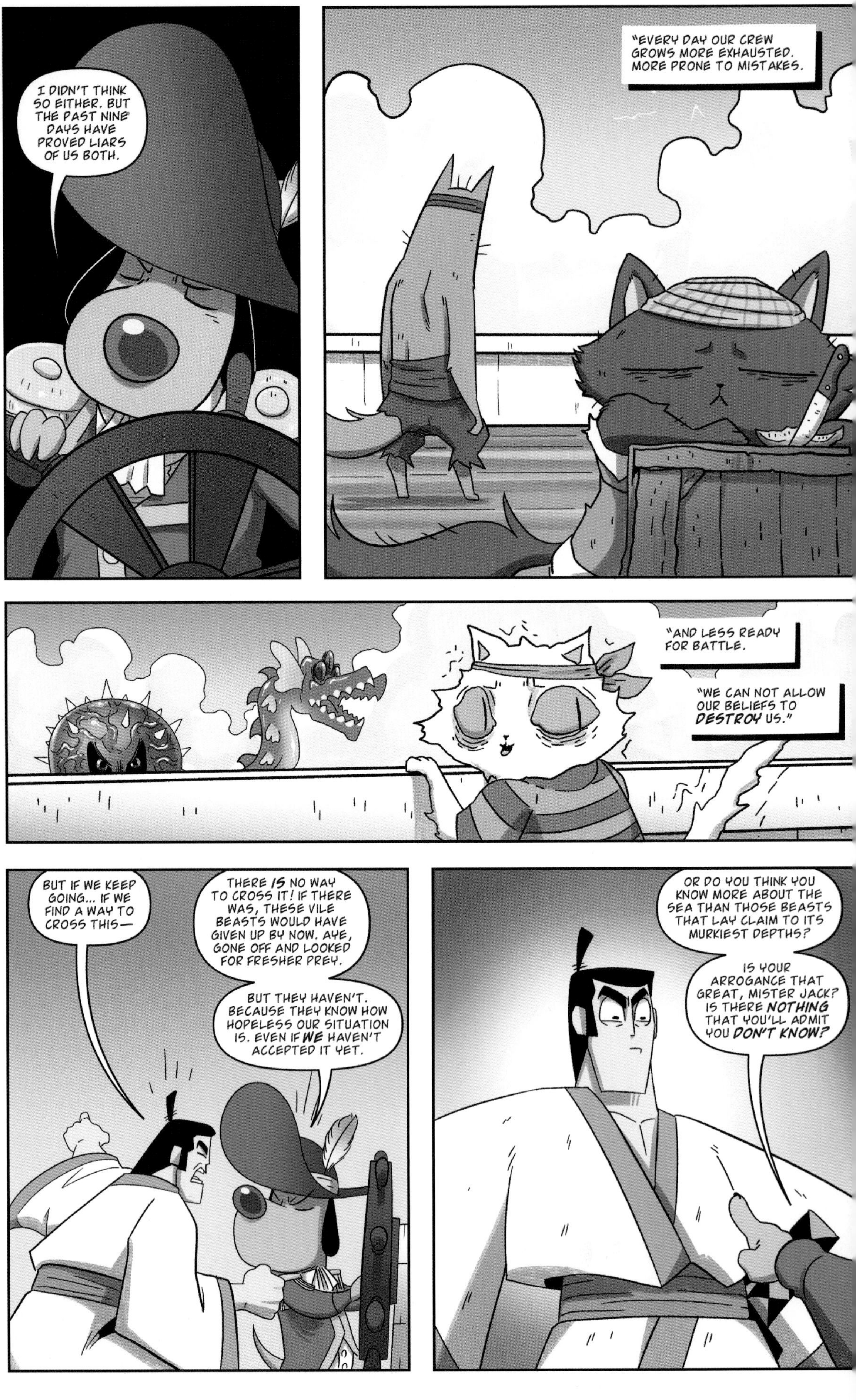
I DIDN'T THINK SO EITHER. BUT THE PAST NINE DAYS HAVE PROVED LIARS OF US BOTH.
"EVERY DAY OUR CREW GROWS MORE EXHAUSTED. MORE PRONE TO MISTAKES.
"AND LESS READY FOR BATTLE.
"WE CAN NOT ALLOW OUR BELIEFS TO DESTROY US."
BUT IF WE KEEP GOING... IF WE FIND A WAY TO CROSS THIS—
THERE IS NO WAY TO CROSS IT! IF THERE WAS, THESE VILE BEASTS WOULD HAVE GIVEN UP BY NOW. AYE, GONE OFF AND LOOKED FOR FRESHER PREY.
BUT THEY HAVEN'T. BECAUSE THEY KNOW HOW HOPELESS OUR SITUATION IS. EVEN IF WE HAVEN'T ACCEPTED IT YET.
OR DO YOU THINK YOU KNOW MORE ABOUT THE SEA THAN THOSE BEASTS THAT LAY CLAIM TO ITS MURKIEST DEPTHS?
IS YOUR ARROGANCE THAT GREAT, MISTER JACK? IS THERE NOTHING THAT YOU'LL ADMIT YOU DON'T KNOW?

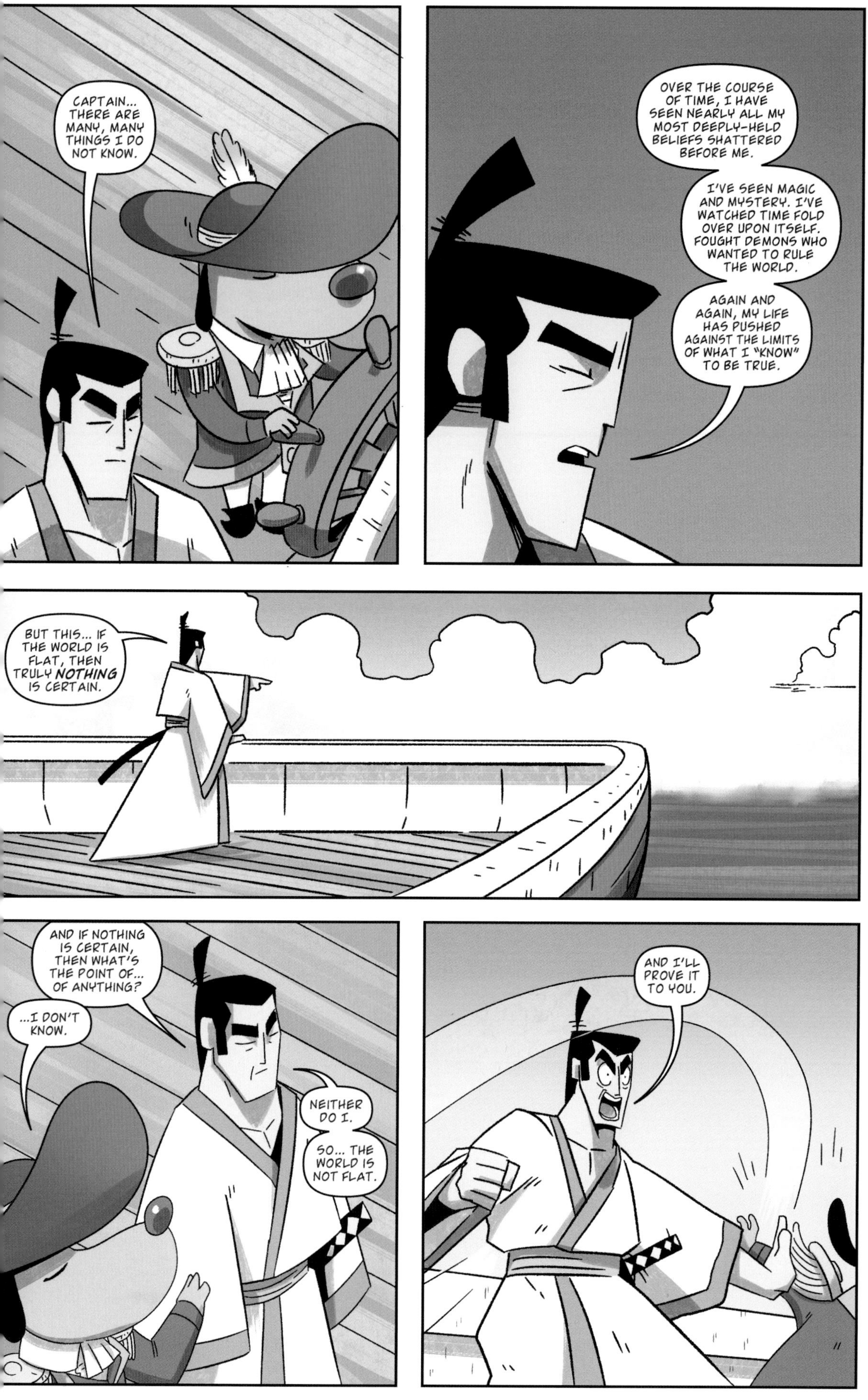
CAPTAIN... THERE ARE MANY, MANY THINGS I DO NOT KNOW.
OVER THE COURSE OF TIME, I HAVE SEEN NEARLY ALL MY MOST DEEPLY-HELD BELIEFS SHATTERED BEFORE ME.
I'VE SEEN MAGIC AND MYSTERY. I'VE WATCHED TIME FOLD OVER UPON ITSELF. FOUGHT DEMONS WHO WANTED TO RULE THE WORLD.
AGAIN AND AGAIN, MY LIFE HAS PUSHED AGAINST THE LIMITS OF WHAT I "KNOW" TO BE TRUE.
BUT THIS... IF THE WORLD IS FLAT, THEN TRULY ***NOTHING*** IS CERTAIN.
AND IF NOTHING IS CERTAIN, THEN WHAT'S THE POINT OF... OF ANYTHING?
...I DON'T KNOW.
NEITHER DO I.
SO... THE WORLD IS NOT FLAT.
AND I'LL PROVE IT TO YOU.

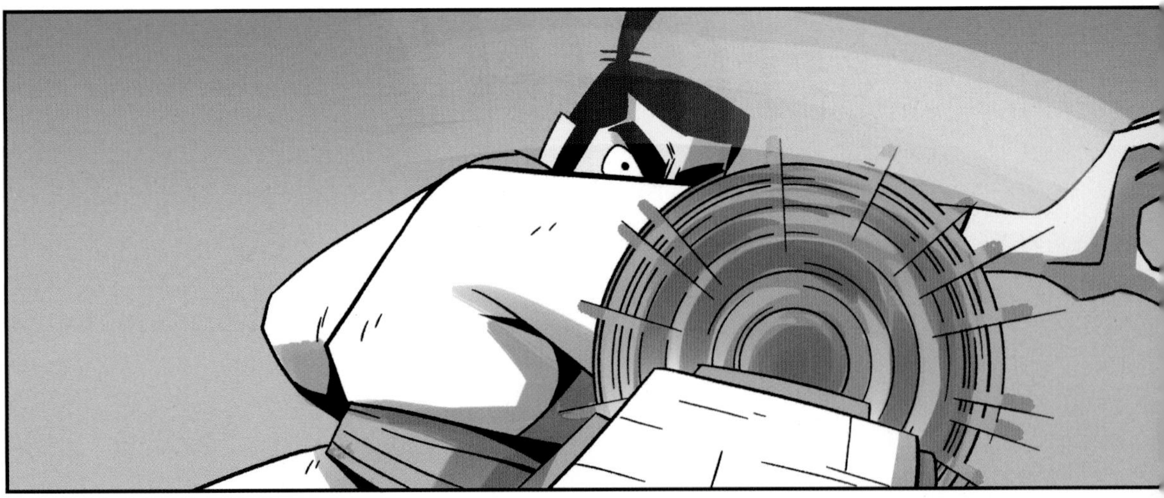

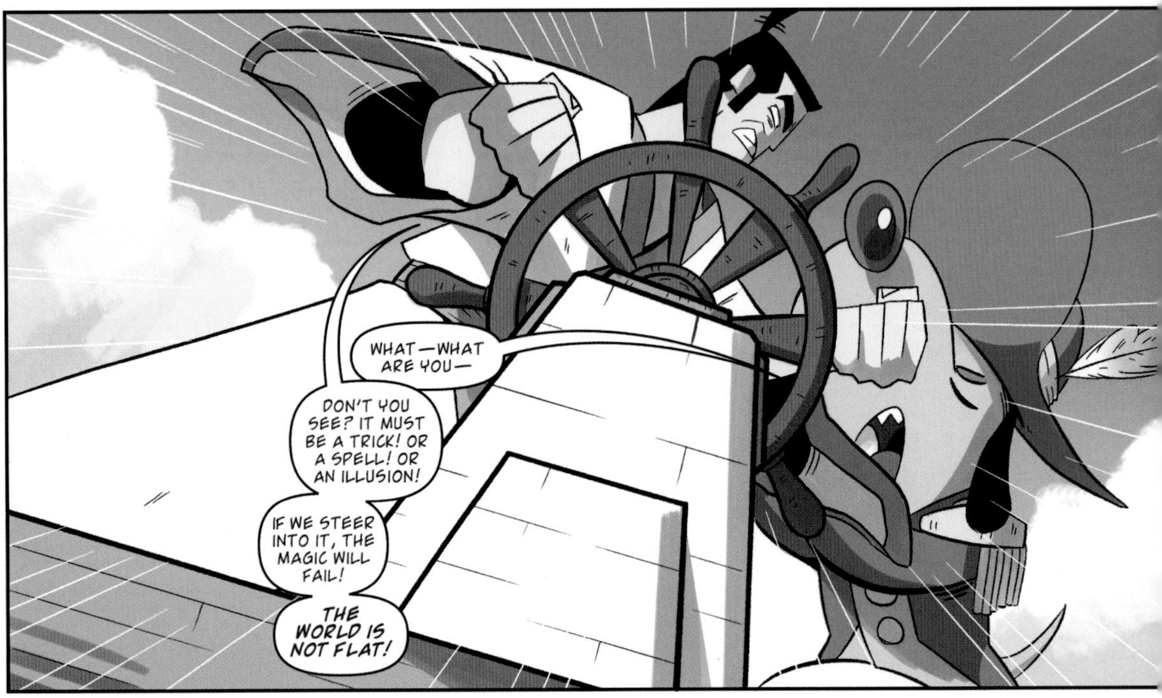
WHAT—WHAT ARE YOU—
DON'T YOU SEE? IT MUST BE A TRICK! OR A SPELL! OR AN ILLUSION!
IF WE STEER INTO IT, THE MAGIC WILL FAIL!
THE WORLD IS NOT FLAT!

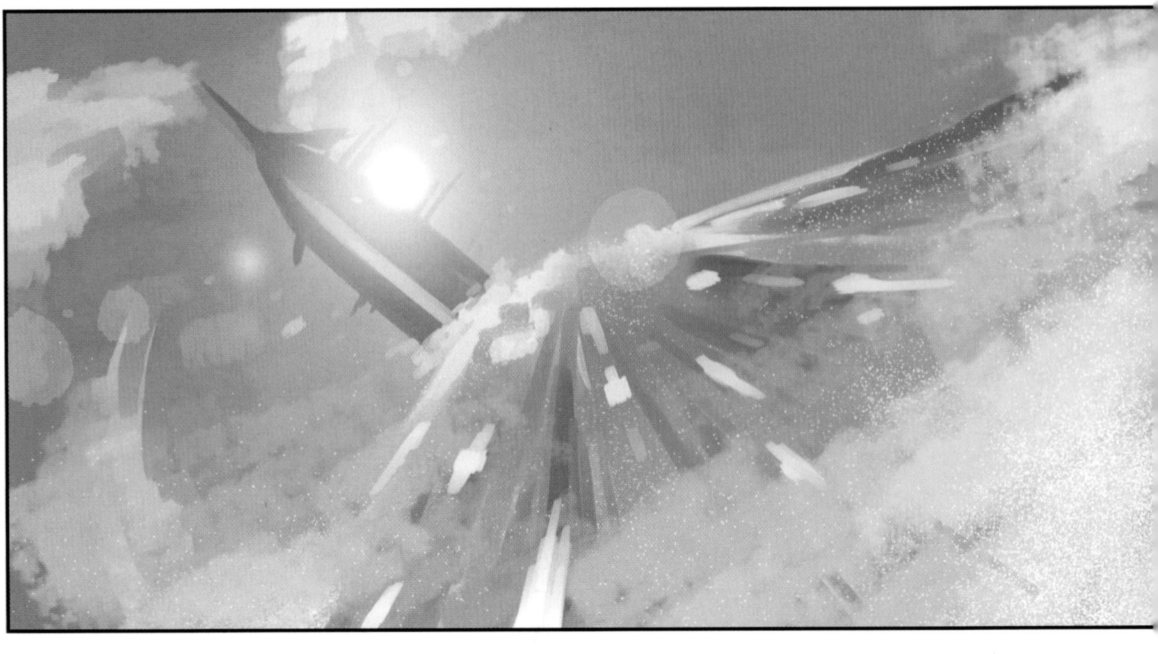

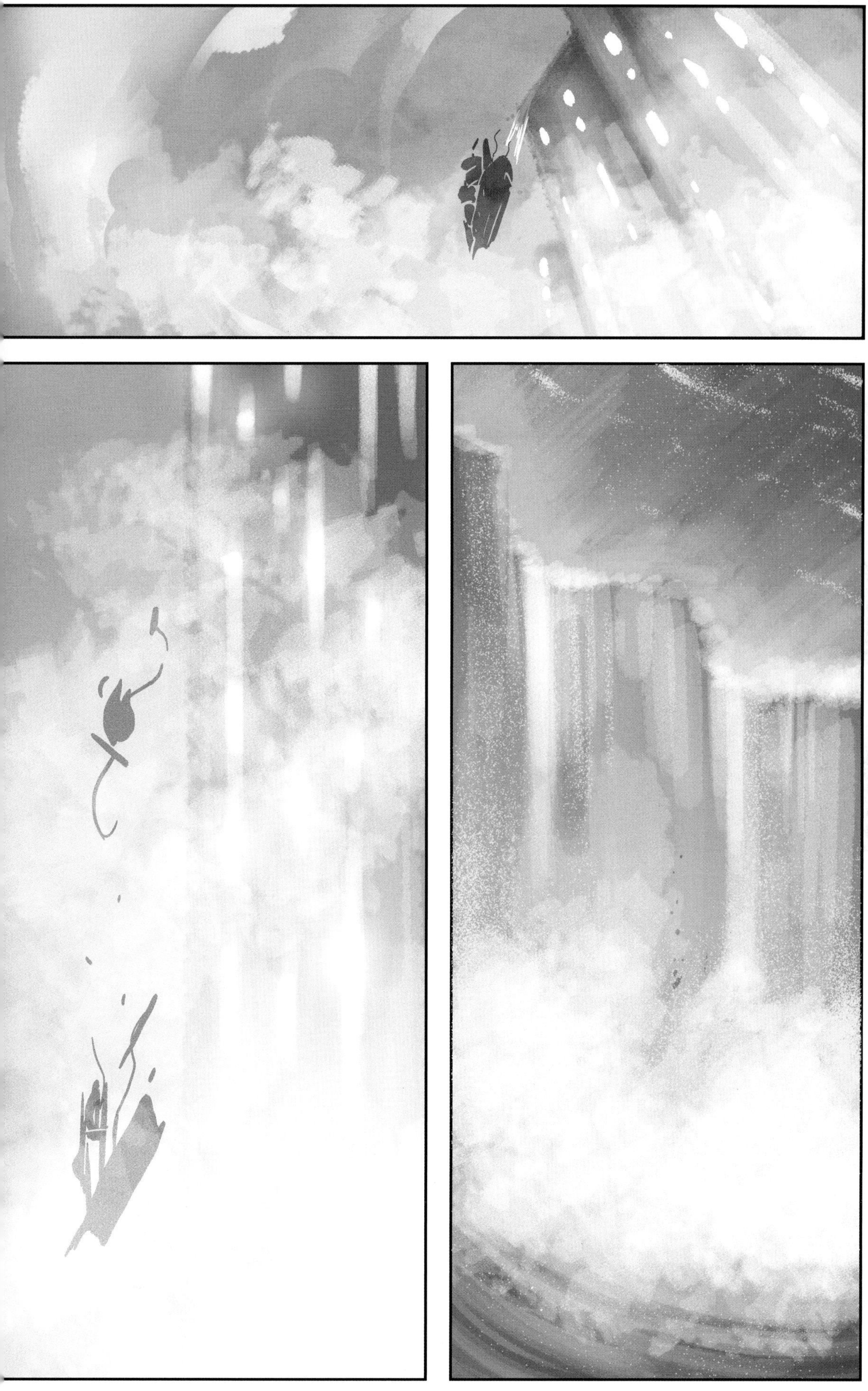

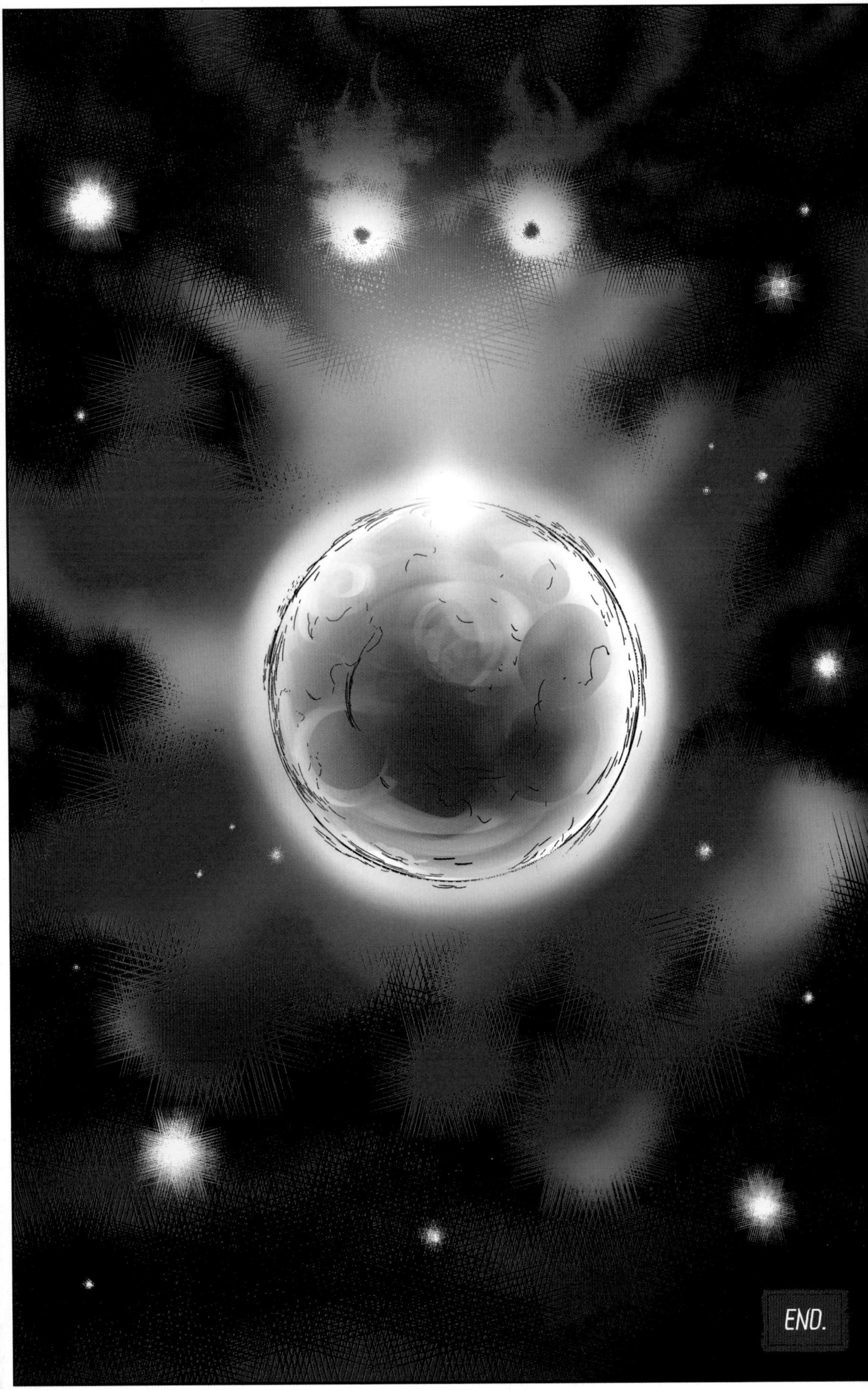
END.

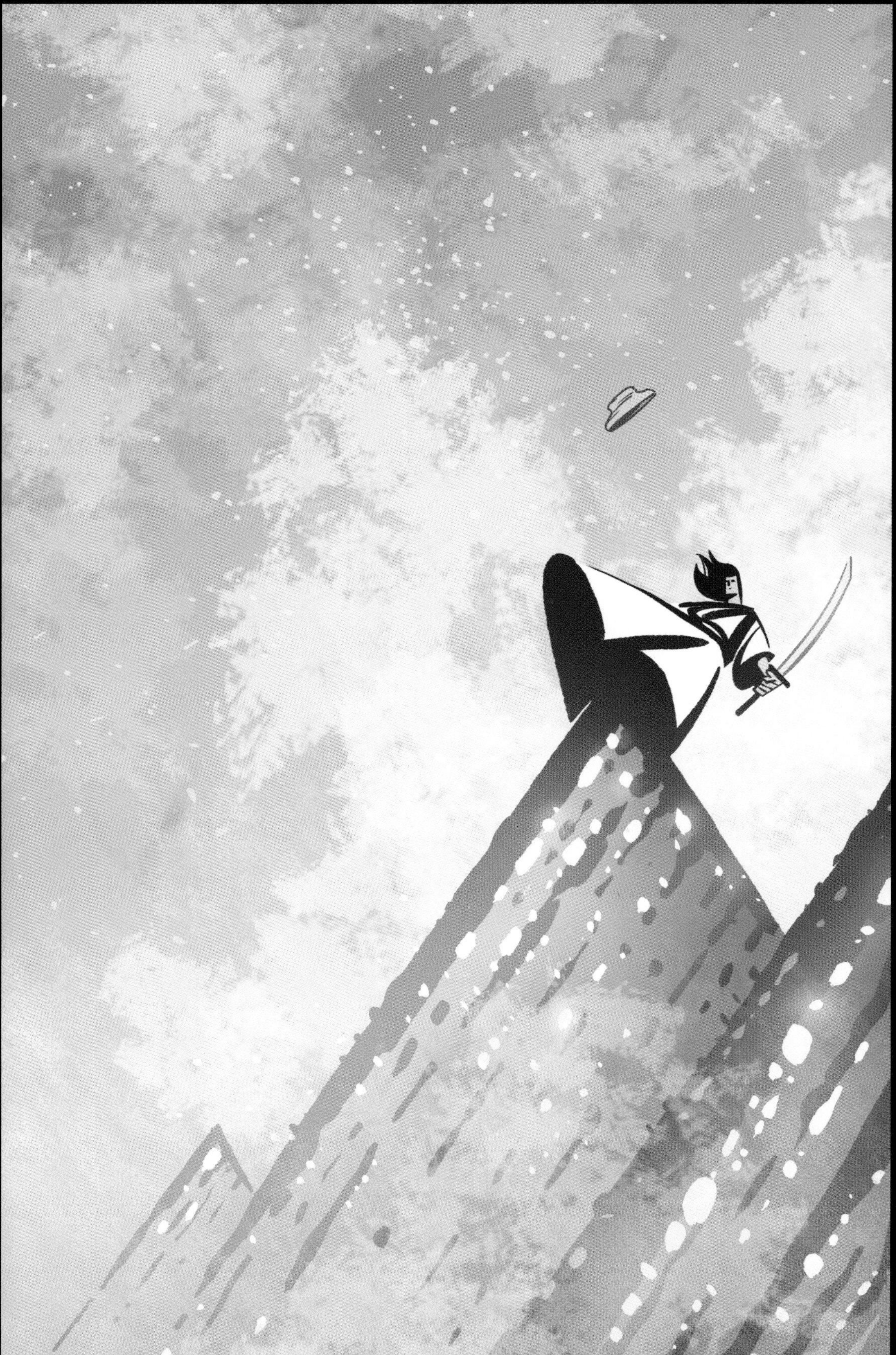

Art by Gavin Fullerton

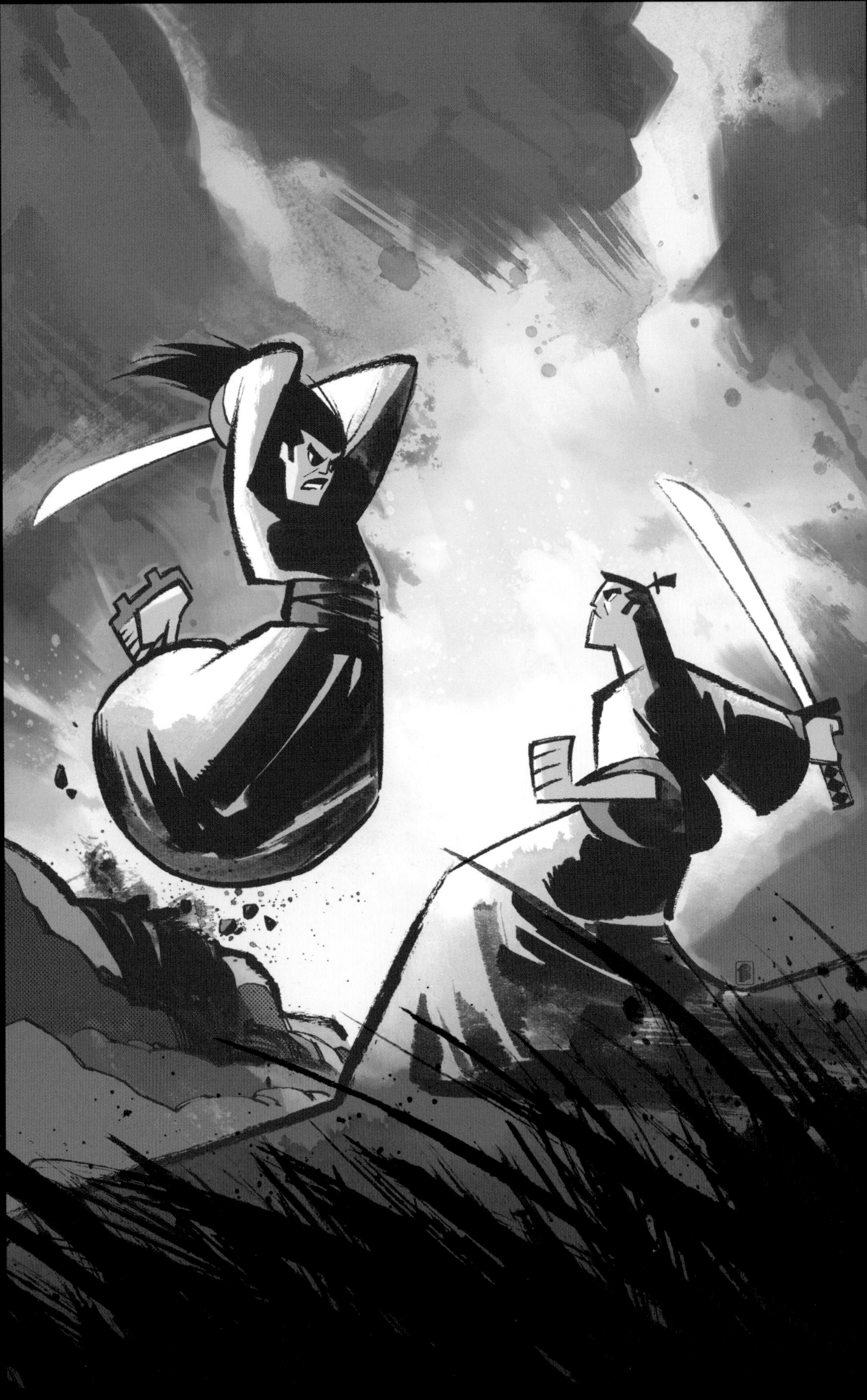

Art by Nelson Dániel

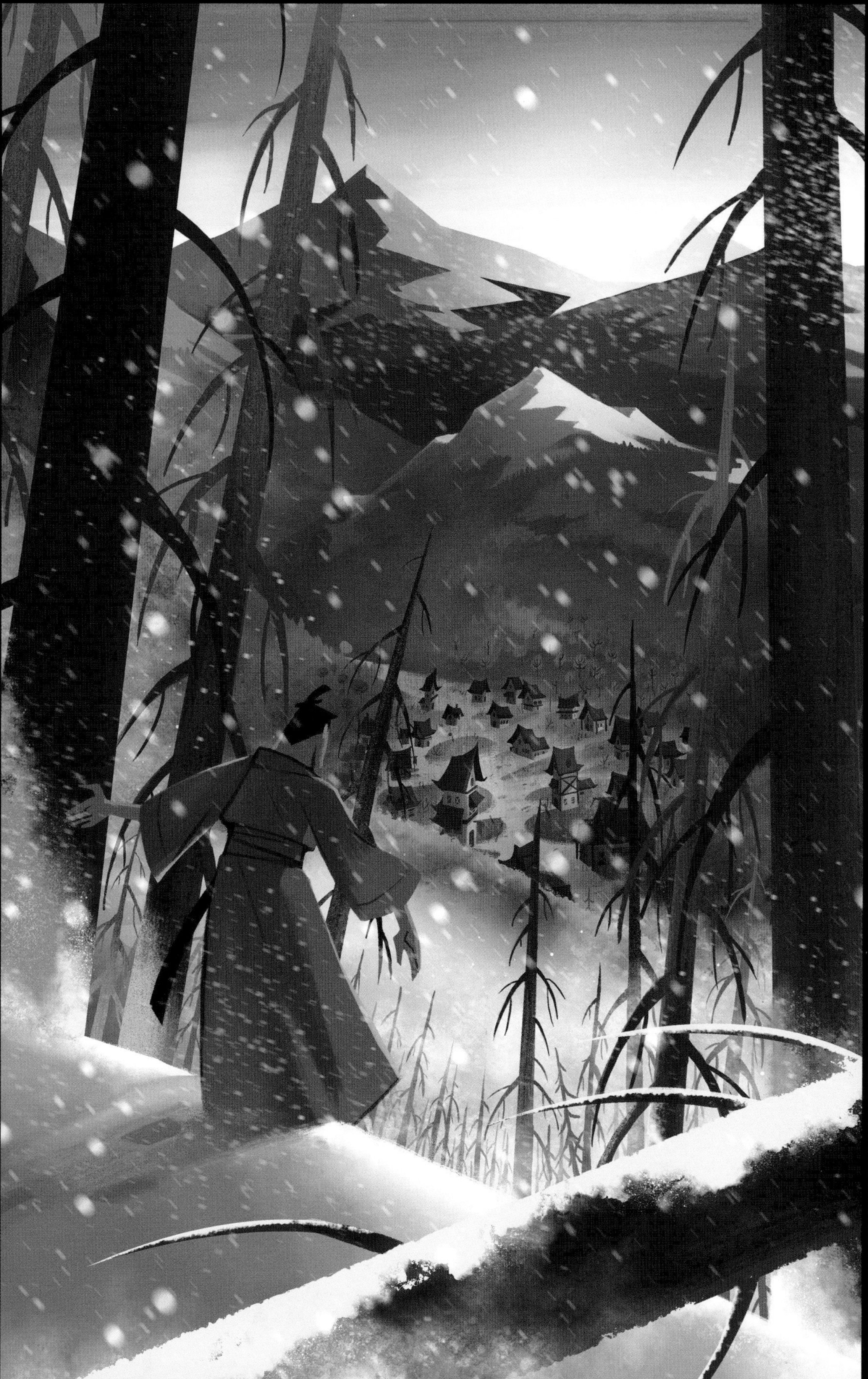

Art by Sara Pitre-Durocher

Art by Kei Zama, Colors by Josh Burcham

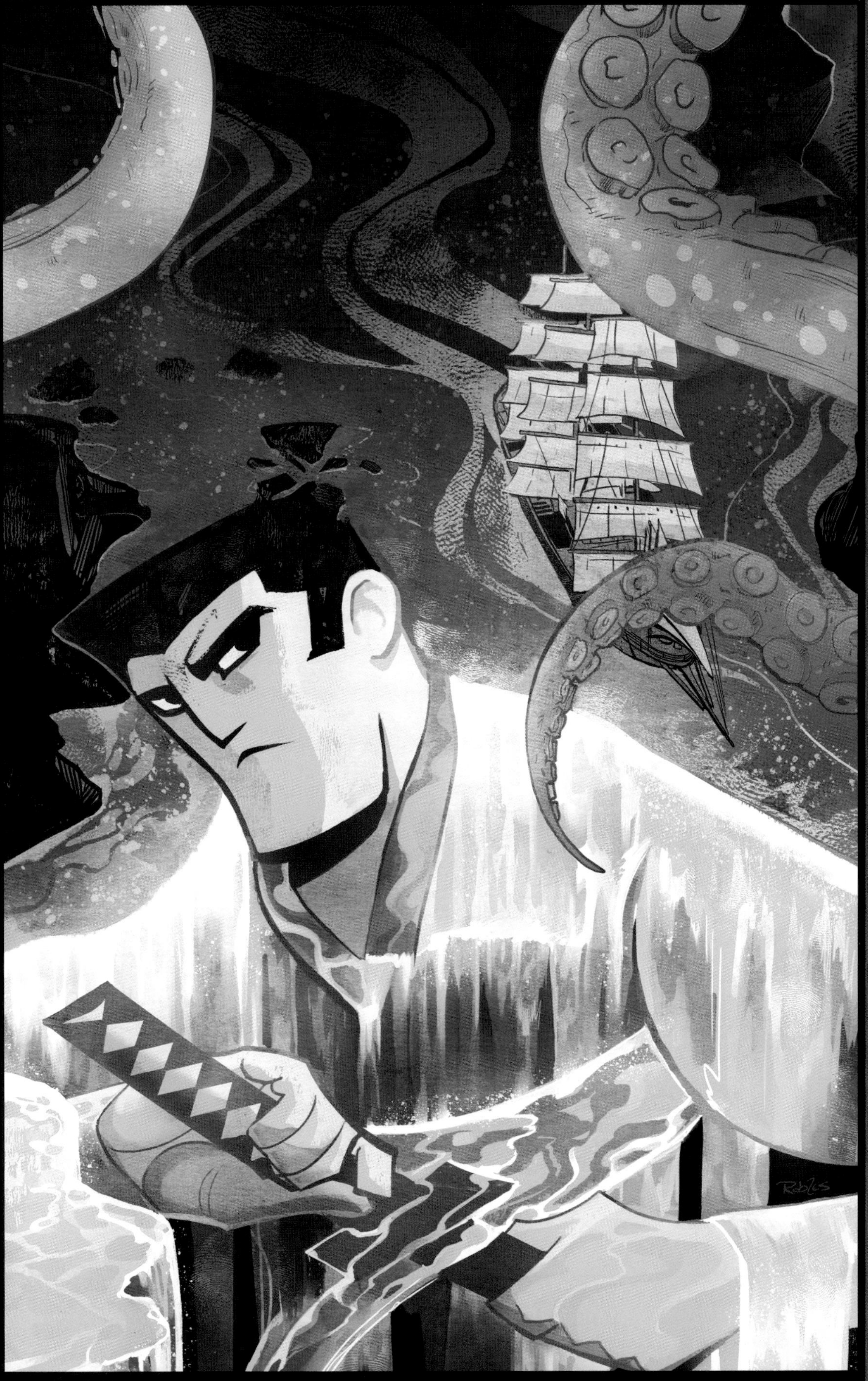
Robles
Art by Nick Robles